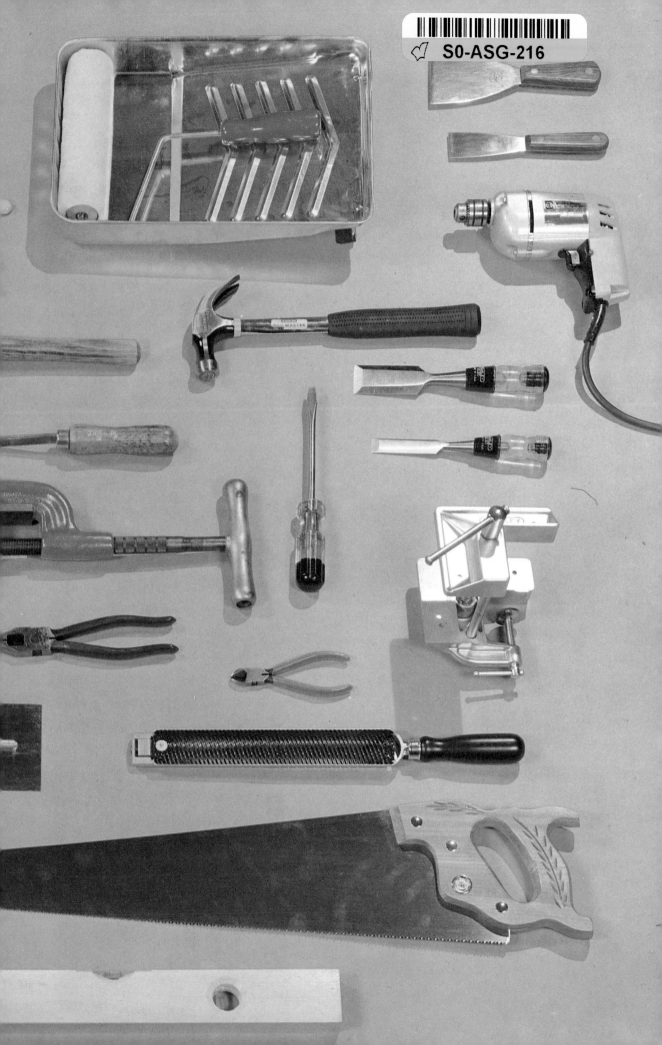

THE
PRACTICAL
HANDYMAN'S
ENCYCLOPEDIA

THE [PRACTICAL] HANDYMAN'S ENCYCLOPEDIA

THE COMPLETE

ILLUSTRATED

[DO IT YOURSELF]

LIBRARY FOR HOME & OUTDOORS

VOLUME TWELVE

GREYSTONE PRESS/NEW YORK · TORONTO · LONDON

CONTENTS FOR VOLUME TWELVE

Use the best method at hand to remove rust from sound surfaces and then prime before repainting.

Rustproof it With Paint

by Richard Day

Cure-alls are yet to come, but here are the things you can do about rust.

EACH YEAR, they figure, rust costs the average family more than $100. This is the toll taken in metal things, mostly iron and steel, around the home that grow to be worth less money each year as corrosion converts them back to the oxides they came from.

Corrosion of metal is a three-legged stool. To have corrosion there must be oxygen, water and electrolytic action. If one of the three is missing, there can be no corrosion. The trouble is that all three are plentiful. Oxygen is in the air. Water is everywhere, practically, even as airborne water vapor. Electrolytic action? That's everywhere too, and it's made worse by things like salt and industrial fumes.

If it were not for the rust-inhibiting primers, fighting corrosion would be a losing battle for homeowners.

The first rust-preventive primers contained lots of red lead. Some still do. Most of the newer ones, however, use zinc chromate, iron oxide, zinc dust, calcium molybdate or basic lead silico chromate pigments. Linseed and tung oil, alkyds, fish oil, acrylic, polyurethane, epoxy, vinyl and other vehicles do the film-forming honors.

Antirust primers work on all three of the conditions for rusting corrosion. The paint films themselves cover the metal, holding moisture and oxygen at bay. More than this, the rust-inhibiting primers fight against the acid conditions that electrolytic action thrives on. Quick as an acid is formed against the metal surface, they neutralize it. Thus, even though small pinholes develop, rust cannot spread.

Most primers for iron and steel contain oils that penetrate rust, locking it to the metal base. There is some benefit to each type of primer. For instance, acrylic primer is a water-thinned latex able to adhere to damp surfaces like sweating pipes, after they're wiped off.

RUST-INHIBITING SYSTEMS

SURFACE	RECOMMENDED COATING	PREPARATION
Unpainted iron and steel	Rust-inhibiting primer Paint to match service	Remove loose rust and scale. Degrease and let dry. Prime with one or two coats, allowing complete drying between. Give one or two coats of paint.
Galvanized metal	Galvanized metal primer Paint to match service	Same as above.
Painted metal	Paint to match service	Degrease. Scrape off blisters, loose rust and peeling paint. Spot-prime bare metal and rust with rust-inhibiting primer. Give one or two coats of paint.
Aluminum, copper	Same as above	Degrease. Oxidized copper must be cleaned by sanding or wire-brushing. Prime, let dry and paint. Oxidized aluminum needs no priming.
Insides of gutters	Bituminous gutter paint	Clean out gutter and let dry. Scrape off rust and brush paint on thickly.

No primer or paint is a cure-all for corrosion. The ideal coating has yet to be developed. However, many paint companies are working on it.

Every bare metal but aluminum, copper and brass needs to be primed before painting. The primer handles the nitty gritty of rust-inhibiting while the top coat keeps the primer intact. Do not leave a primer exposed to the weather for more than a month. Paint over it as soon as it's dry.

Galvanized Metal Primers

You once had to let galvanized steel weather for six months or else acid-etch it before you could paint it successfully. Not so, now. Special primers, some of them containing zinc dust, are designed for direct application to degreased galvanized metal. Ordinary metal primers used on galvanized metal are likely to flake off within a short time. Zinc-dust-containing primers need frequent stirring to keep the pigment from settling.

Surface Preparation

Even more than in painting wood, surface preparation is an important part of painting metal.

Metal surfaces should be clean, free of dirt, salt, grease and oil. Use a wire brush, sandpaper, scraper, power sander or electric drill with wire brush attachment to take off loose paint, mill scale and rust. While the best job of preparation would remove all deposits down to bright metal, if you remove all *loose* rust and scale, you can get by. Oily deposits can be removed by cleaning thoroughly with trisodium phosphate (TSP), turpentine or paint thinner solvents. TSP should be rinsed off thoroughly. If an old paint is flaked, it may have to be removed. Prime immediately.

Surfaces that are contaminated with salt, such as those found along coastal areas, need a thorough wash-down with hot water, then a rinse. Prime as soon as dry. If it is long between priming and painting, another washing may be needed.

Galvanized metal gutters can be painted without weathering or acid-etching with special primer.

Generous coat of rot-proof gutter paint on the inside will help give it bonus years of service.

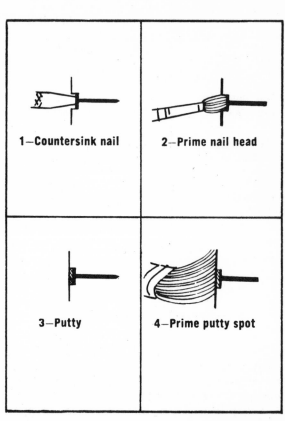

Rust-Oleum Corp.

A power sander saves lots of work in preparing metal for priming. Removes loose rust, old paint.

Countersink iron nails with nail set, dab on a bit of prime, putty hole, then prime with paint.

1—Countersink nail

2—Prime nail head

3—Putty

4—Prime putty spot

Author found that short, cone-shaped roller was handy tool for repainting his galvanized flashing.

Prevent rust on lower three inches of furnace by painting with a rust-inhibiting paint as shown.

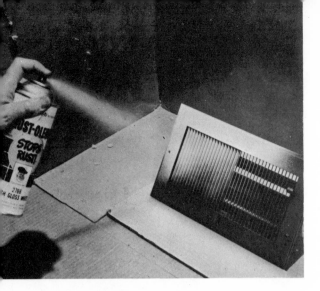

Heating system parts will rust even indoors. Use rust-inhibitive primer, paint to match the decor.

Rust-Oleum photos

Besides protection from rust, metal stair rails need hard-wear coat that can withstand weather.

A flat applicator is one of the easiest ways to wipe antirust paint onto screens that need it.

Old painted surfaces, on which the paint film is intact, can be repainted without priming, merely by cleaning and sanding the old finish. If the old paint is chalked excessively, then an overall primer coat is called for. Areas where the bare metal is exposed should be spot-primed.

For maximum protection, two priming coats can be given. Flow the primer on heavily. The thicker you can get it on without runs, the better. Most manufacturers do not recommend painting metal when the temperature is below 50°F.

Slow-corroding metals such as aluminum and copper need not be painted if the normal aluminum oxide gray color and the normal green copper oxide color are not objectionable. The oxide coating on aluminum in an excellent base for paint.

The Paints Themselves

The antirust paints, designed as part of rust-inhibiting systems, are usually similar in formulation to primers. However, they withstand weathering better and are available in a number of colors.

Once a metal has been primed properly any paint may be put on it, latex included. The finish coat should match the service it will see. Some manufacturers recommend putting their regular high-gloss enamels over rust-preventive primers. Latex serves well for non-wear uses while a shovel or lawnmower would require an enamel.

A special kind of rust-preventive paint is designed just for use on the insides of gutters. Bituminous-based, it is effective on both wood and metal gutters.

The rust-preventive paints may be applied by brush, roller or spray. Many are available in aerosol form.

If yours is going to be one household where rust gets short-changed on its $100 claim this year, don't forget that rusting isn't confined to outdoor metal. Some indoor metal needs protecting too. •

Fine Inside Finishes

Painting indoors the new, easy way is nothing but a sweet smellin' breeze.

Flat latex paint goes on ceilings easily. Overlap each stroke of roller about one third previous one.

Paint in laundry areas takes much abuse. Epoxy-type enamels are the ideal finish for these areas, even though they cost more than the other paints.

A SMELLY HOUSE, a mess to clean up and a week or two with paint-speckled fingers used to be the name of the game when painting a room. Not so today. Paint technology has come to the rescue. With a gallon or so of latex flat paint and about a quart of matching semigloss latex enamel you can paint the walls and trim in an entire room of average size for less than $10. There's nothing but a pleasant smell. Clean-up is with water, and you can often do the job in one coat in part of a day.

While flat latex wall paint has most of the desirable characteristics of an interior paint, it lacks the water resistance necessary for frequent washing. Also lacking is the resistance to wear that some uses call for. For this reason semigloss latex enamel is recommended for woodwork because woodwork wears faster, gets dirty sooner and must be washed more often.

The use of a room also has a bearing on the finish that is best for it. While ceilings and walls look best with a flat finish, these tend to hold onto soil and are thus not very washable. For that reason, walls and ceilings in the three hard-use rooms—bath, kitchen and laundry—should have a glossy or at least a semiglossy finish.

The hardest uses of all occur next to the kitchen stove, near the laundry tub and next to bathtubs and showers. If extreme toughness and soap and detergent resistance is needed in these locations, one of the new epoxy-type enamels should be used.

The Paints

While many different paints may be used on the interior of a house, all are not

Dressed for painting, this smart home handywoman knows that skin is easier to clean than clothes.

INTERIOR PAINTING SYSTEMS

SURFACE	RECOMMENDED PAINT	EXCEPTIONS AND ALTERNATES
Living room, bedroom, dining room, hallway, walls and ceilings	Latex paint	Semi-gloss enamel is better for rooms where activities may soil walls; i.e., nursery, narrow hallways, stairways, etc. Extra-flat types may be used for ceilings.
Trim and woodwork	Semi-gloss latex enamel	Regular latex paint may be used on trim as well as walls if soiling is minimal. Also suitable are semi-gloss oil-base enamel or alkyd. Gloss enamel may be used if the shiny surface is not objectionable.
Kitchen, laundry, bathroom walls, ceilings and trim	Semi-gloss latex enamel	Semi-gloss enamel may be used in bathrooms, but gloss enamel is preferable.
Around stoves, tubs, showers where extreme water, grease and detergent resistance is desired	Epoxy-type enamels	Cost is higher but they're worth it for long life and easy maintenance. Can be used on the entire room.
Wood floors	Epoxy floor enamel	Oil-base floor enamel may be used to save on cost, but repainting at intervals will be necessary.

equally good for the job. For best results and the easiest paints to use follow the recommendations in the chart on interior painting systems.

Latex flat wall paint—Thins and cleans up with water. Dries quickly in one or two hours ready to recoat. Some are designed for one-coat coverage; others need two. Easy to apply. Doesn't show touch-up or lap marks. Dries to flat or velvety sheen. Needs no primer over any clean, non-glossy surface. Pleasant smell. Water and wear resistance is poor. Limited mostly to light colors.

Semigloss latex enamel—This spanking new coating has all the advantages of a latex paint and produces a tough, washable finish. It's good for kitchens and baths as well as for woodwork and trim.

Dripless latex—Recently developed, dripless latex paint is designed especially for use on ceilings. Normal latex paint is made jelly-like with a thickening agent to keep it from running off the brush or roller. Use dripless paint if you wish, but don't count on it as a cure-all for spattering. If you roll too fast, even dripless paint will mist from the roller. Cover your furniture and floor, dripless or not.

Enamel—Takes hard wear, especially in the glossy finish. Resistant to detergents, greases and water. Available in all colors. Clean-up is with paint thinner or turpentine. Has painty smell. More difficult to apply. Needs overnight to dry for recoating.

Alkyd—Sticks to almost any surface. Resists wear and has fair water resistance. Good for woodwork. Self-priming. Covers in one or two coats. Little odor. One paint can be used for both walls and trim. Needs clean-up with paint thinner or turpentine. Flat finish should be used. Needs to dry overnight for recoat.

Texture paints—These thick-bodied coatings may be desirable to camouflage a carload of sins, such as poor plasterboard joint-taping, and scarred walls or for their texture. Available in latex or oil-base, with or without sand for added texture, they may be applied with brush or roller. Texture is created by rolling or tooling while still wet. Coverage is only about 25 square feet per quart, but the cost is low too. Texture paints don't wash well. Either avoid them for kitchens, baths and laundry areas or coat them with a sealer, then with a semigloss enamel.

Epoxy—One of the most water-, grease- and wear-resistant paints made. Usually two parts are mixed to activate. Must be

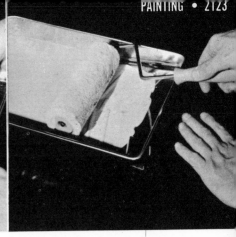

When you have finally decided what color to use and have prepared the area for the application of the paint, fill roller tray's well about half full of paint. Pick up paint on roller by rolling it in well. Even out paint on roller by rolling it several times up and down on tray's sloped end.

used within a limited time after mixing. Clean-up is with epoxy thinner. Available in a range of colors. Cost is high, application is with brush, roller or spray.

Casein—Not recommended. This paint has been shot down by the newer, better types.

Calcimine—Cheapest paint made. Forget about it.

Floor enamel—Tough-clinging, hard-wearing paint for wood, metal and some other surfaces on floors and stairs. Self-priming.

Epoxy floor enamel—Practically indestructible finish for wood, metal, concrete and other floors above or below ground. Immune to grease and gasoline. Resists alkali and water damage. Costs more than regular floor enamel.

Pigmented shellac primer-sealer—Rates special mention for nearly all interior priming and sealing because it dries within minutes, primes white and seals. This multipurpose material kills stains, covers knots, seals sap streaks and hides grease marks. Often by the time you finish priming, the first-coated area is ready to be painted. Brush and roller texture show-through is a problem, though, because fast-drying prevents full leveling. Use under latex, alkyd or oil paints. Don't use it outdoors.

How Much Paint?

A few quick measurements will tell you how much paint is needed for the job. You needn't be exact . . . to the nearest foot will do. Nothing does it like a yardstick.

Figure for wall paint by multiplying room height by the distance around the outside of a room (around all four walls). Divide that by 125. (Most interior paints will cover about 125 square feet per quart.)

This gives the number of quarts of wall paint needed. Don't deduct for window and door openings unless they're especially large.

To figure how many quarts of paint are needed for the ceiling, multiply room length by room width and divide the result by 125. If walls and ceiling are to be painted with the same paint, add the totals together before ordering paint.

Paint for woodwork is usually different from wall paint. Get about one fourth as much for trim as for walls.

Painting a Room

Preparation, the paint cats say, is the most important step in painting any room. Start by removing curtains, drapes and venetian blinds. Move furniture, putting everything in the center of the room and covering it with a dropcloth. Old sheets will do. Cover the floor with newspapers to protect it.

See that wall and woodwork surfaces are free of dirt, grease and wax that might interfere with paint adhesion. Remove all traces of wax by wiping with a turpentine-soaked cloth. Kitchen and bathroom walls can rarely be painted without washing. Use detergent and water to get rid of grease film and soap and water spots. Rinse well. Even the no-rinse cleaners should be rinsed before painting.

Washing the other rooms isn't necessary unless they badly need it. Rather than wash a wall, some homeowners paint it to cover up the dirt. Painting is easier than washing, they figure.

Any loose or broken plaster should be repaired with patching plaster, allowed to dry and sanded smooth. Spot-prime patches with an extra coat of latex paint, if that's the finishing system you will use.

Make sure tray and roller, if used—are clean.

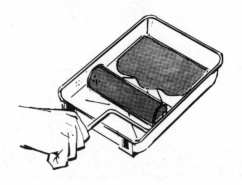

Before starting—make sure you have right roller.

Start with ceiling. Apply in "W" to distribute.

Roll in different directions to spread the paint.

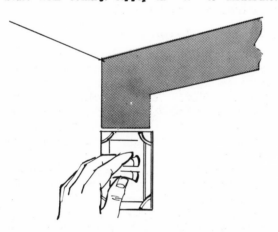

A sponge pad is handy for painting into corners.

Apply in "W" to walls, cross-spread it sideways.

Squeegee excess paint onto papers when finished.

Wash out latex from roller and tray under faucet.

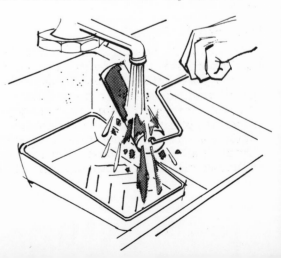

Use a brush to cut in at corners, doors and wall openings. Fill between with roller, shown, left.

Patch any nicks, scrapes or cracks in walls with spackling compound using a putty knife. Hairline cracks are best filled by rubbing soupy spackle back and forth across the crack with your finger.

Remove all hardware from doors and windows. Either loosen light fixtures and let them hang down slightly or mask them. Take off electrical switch and receptacle covers. If they are to be painted, put these where you'll remember to do it. Dust the walls with a cloth, dust mop or tack rag and you are ready to paint.

Applying the Paint

Even before you open a can of paint read the label thoroughly. Follow the instructions to the letter.

Some paints should not be stirred just before applying them. The label will tell you.

Start applying paint at the ceiling. To prevent lap marks work across the width of the room in strips, narrow ones if you're using any but a latex paint. If possible, paint the whole ceiling at once.

The easiest way to paint a ceiling is with a long-handled roller. A ladder is needed only for cutting in the edges.

Start painting a wall in the upper left corner, in vertical strips to prevent lap marks. For roller painting cut in the corners and around openings with a 2-inch brush. Don't try to do all the cutting in at once unless you are using a latex paint. It's those lap marks, again.

Wipe up any spatters or spills as you go, especially when using a fast-drying paint such as a latex.

Painting Woodwork

Paint the woodwork last, using the proper paint for it.

Some enamels used on woodwork are too glossy to provide good bond for a new finish. Before painting, these surfaces should be roughened. Either sand them with 6/0 paper or apply a surface conditioner to remove the gloss. As added help apply an enamel undercoat. It will introduce one finish to the other, thus cutting down on the amount of sanding that is needed.

If the old paint is thickly built up, chipping is sure to shoot down your new paint job. To prevent it the old paint should be removed before repainting. Refinish as with new wood. Likewise, when varnished woodwork is to be painted in order to make a room look larger and more modern, chipping can be a problem. The varnish should be taken off.

A prevalent problem in painting wood trim is elimination of brush marks. These are caused by use of a brush that is too stiff, by brushing too hard or by brushing after the paint has begun to set. Brush marks from previous paint jobs will show through if they are not sanded down. Use 6/0 paper.

Painting Windows

Painting windows calls for patience and a steady hand. You can save your ulcer by masking the window first, but be sure to remove the masking tape before it gets baked onto the glass. You can either wipe off spatters on the glass while they're wet or scrape them off later with a razor blade. It's a toss-up.

Paint a double-hung window by first adjusting it so that the lower part of the upper sash can be painted. Then raise the upper sash almost to the top and finish painting it. Paint the lower sash with it slightly raised. Paint the recessed part of the window frame next, then the frame and finally the sill.

Painting Doors

On doors, paint the frame first, then the top, back and front edges of the door itself. If it's a paneled door, paint the panels and panel molding next, starting at the top. Wipe off any paint that gets on the area around the panels. Finally paint the rest of the door, from top down.

New Surfaces

If you are painting a new room addition or working with previously unpainted materials, you'll need to take additional steps to be sure of a lasting job. Here are the various surfaces and the steps needed:

New Plaster—Unless painting with latex paint, new plaster should be thoroughly dry—60 to 90 days drying is recommended. Latex paints may be put on fresh plaster as soon as it is hard enough for the trim to be nailed. One coat will serve as a primer, the other for a cover coat.

Plasterboard—Be sure that plasterboard panels are well nailed to the studs. Nails should be slightly dimpled into the surface, but without breaking the paper covering. Panel joints must be taped, smoothed with joint compound and sanded before painting. Paint will not hide them otherwise. Prime and paint plasterboard the same as plaster.

New Wood—Fill nail holes, joints and cracks. Sand smooth with 6/0 paper to keep patched areas from showing through the paint. Most manufacturers say that latex paints should not be put on bare wood without priming to seal the wood pores and keep water in the paint from raising the grain. Other paints may not need primers on bare wood. Consult the label.

Plywood—For latex paint seal, then paint with one or two coats. For other paints on plywood, prime and follow with one or two color coats.

Hardboard—Either standard or tempered hardboards, such as *Masonite*, may be primed with any undercoat that is recommended for wood. This will seal their porous surfaces. First be sure that the panels are clean. Sanded areas and those roughened during shipping will need two coats of primer. Some hardboards are factory-primed and may be painted directly with any type of interior paint.

Wallpaper—When firm and even, wallpaper may be painted over. That's good! No, that's bad. You'll curse your rotten judgment if you ever need to remove painted-over wallpaper. Before painting wallpaper, if you must, see that loose edges are pasted down. If wallpaper is greasy, clean it with wallpaper cleaner. When

Test fresh plaster to see if it is dry enough to paint by striking match. If match lights, it's dry.

PAINTING WINDOWS

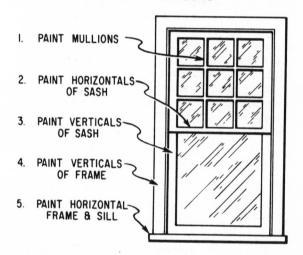

1. PAINT MULLIONS
2. PAINT HORIZONTALS OF SASH
3. PAINT VERTICALS OF SASH
4. PAINT VERTICALS OF FRAME
5. PAINT HORIZONTAL FRAME & SILL

Follow this scheme in painting windows to make the job go faster and eliminate skipping spots.

using a latex paint over wallpaper, test an area to be sure the paint doesn't soften the wallpaper paste and cause peeling.

Insulation Board—Often used for ceiling tile, insulation board is made from cellulose fibers that are tightly pressed together. It is quite porous. Sometimes a factory-applied finish seals the board, but it's tough to tell without putting on some paint. If there is any doubt, apply one coat of oil-base primer-sealer. Watch to see if this dries to a uniform surface. If it does, the board is sealed. If not, a second coat is needed. Finish can be with any wall paint.

Some insulation boards are asphalt-impregnated and must be stabilized with specially recommended sealers to prevent bleeding.

Ceramic Tile—Ceramic tile that is discolored or damaged, can be painted to look like new with epoxy paints. Its color can

When using oil-base paints, roller tray cleaning can be bad news. To eliminate problems, slip a plastic cleaner's bag over tray, press to fit before filling. When finished, pull off the bag and discard it

Teamwork always gets the job done faster—even on the same small area. Here we see the man doing the delicate sash using a cardboard guide while the wife paints the window trim. Small brushes used.

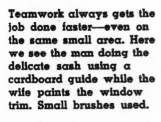

Painting over wallpaper looks like a great idea, but it is a serious step. Once you do it, the paper will be extremely tough to remove if so desired.

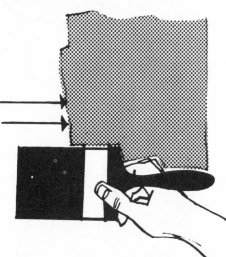

When using a brush (or a roller) always start to paint in the farthest, unpainted area you are about to cover and work into the area just previously covered to prevent lap marks. Paint ceiling in strips, starting in corner. Don't reach too far.

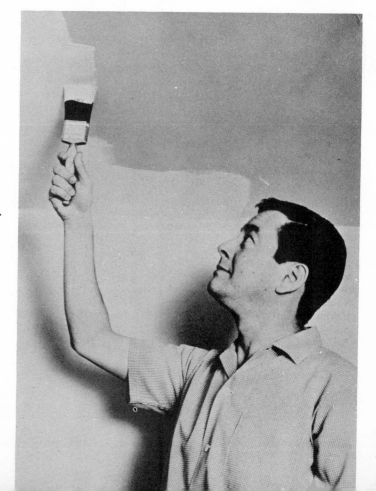

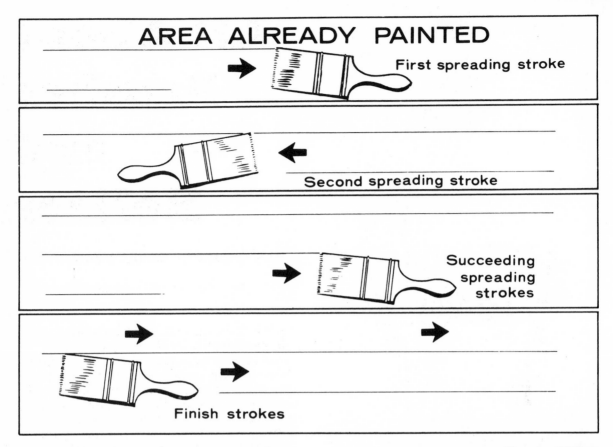

AREA ALREADY PAINTED

First spreading stroke

Second spreading stroke

Succeeding spreading strokes

Finish strokes

Sherman-Williams

To paint with a brush, then, dip it about half-way into paint. Spread first in one direction, then in the other. Make succeeding spreading strokes all in one direction, blending the new paint into that on area already painted. The finish strokes should be light, long and straight.

Water thinned paints may be washed out of your brushes under faucet. Work bristles thoroughly.

be changed too, if desired, by painting. Repair cracked or chipped tile and regrout open areas. Use a brush or mohair roller and apply one coat of paint to the thoroughly cleaned, degreased tile. The next day you can use a paint-striping tool and white paint to put the joint lines back on the surface. The effect is very much like the original ceramic tile wall when it was new.

Plastic Tile—Apply a coat of pigmented shellac primer-sealer to the well cleaned, repaired tile. Follow with an enamel undercoat, sand lightly when dry. Dust well and put on a finishing coat of semi-gloss or gloss enamel.

If you take the few extra hours that are needed to cover every step in the proper painting procedure inside your house, the job should last for years. By the time you're ready for another repainting, you'll be ready for a change in color anyway. •

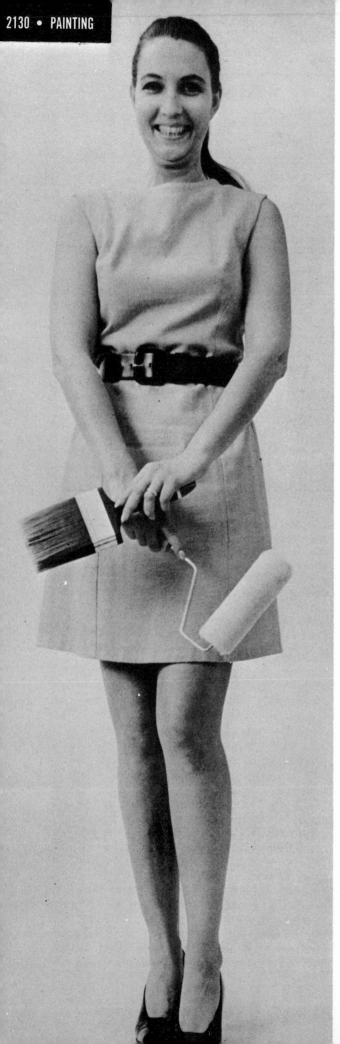

All About Brushes and Rollers

Usually used in combination, roller for flat areas, brush for trim.

THE TWO BASIC painting tools are the paint brush and the paint roller. A brush soaks up paint between its bristles. When drawn across a surface to be painted, the paint slides out and is deposited on the surface in a thin film. A roller soaks up paint in its nap. When the roller is wheeled across a surface to be painted, paint is squeezed out and left on the surface in a thin film.

Which method you use depends on the job. Large flat expanses of wall and ceiling favor the use of a roller for its speed. Detail and trim painting favor the brush for its greater maneuverability. Painters sometimes use a combination of the two: a roller for flat expanses and a brush for trim. However, with some paints this may leave you with two different textures unless the right roller is chosen to produce a smooth brush-like finish.

Brushes

A good paint brush that is cared for properly will last many years. But few handymen will ever use a brush until it wears out. Very few. Most brushes become useless through neglect of one sort or another.

Some of the finest paint brushes are made with imported hog bristles, which are *flagged,* or split at the ends to help them hold and spread paint. Unless they're the tough-bristle kind like calcimine brushes, these natural-bristle brushes should not be used with water-thinned paints. The bristles are so porous they swell and get

Whether you use a brush or a roller for the job, get a good one. Then proceed—with confidence.

Use the largest brush that is practical for the job. A four-inch brush is ideal for wall work.

soggy in water. You know how hogs hate to take baths.

When buying a natural bristle brush get the undyed kind. The label would read, "100% undyed natural bristle." They're cheaper and just as good. There is no reason why a brush has to be black.

Some synthetic bristles equal or surpass natural bristles for most painting. They're cheaper too. Usually nylon, these bristles have their ends artificially flagged or exploded to make them act like hog bristles in applying paint. Synthetic bristle brushes are ideal for applying water-thinned paints. Moreover, they outwear natural-bristle brushes.

Bristle length affects the cost of a paint brush. While long bristles cost more, they hold more paint than short bristles. Remember this when you buy.

Don't judge a good brush by the stock of less-than-a-dollar brushes sold in all too many stores. Cheap brushes hold little paint. They won't produce a smooth finish and they leave unsightly brush marks. With a cheap brush you soon tire of brushing. But they *are* cheap. Use them for throw-away-type work.

A good brush has many benefits: Its bristles are set securely into the ferrule in rubber or epoxy. The chance of it shedding bristles to bomb out your paint job is small. A good brush picks up plenty of paint. This means you dip less often and work faster, with less effort. Paint goes on smoothly. There is little drag or pull. You get a more uniform, better looking paint job with fewer strokes and less arm weariness. A good brush makes paint go further because it spreads evenly. At the same time, it helps paint to bond better with the surface, providing a more durable, longer lasting finish.

A good brush is made better to last longer. While it costs from $8 to $20, a good brush can make painting a pleasure. If you want professional results, invest in a professional brush. If there is a single secret to successful painting, a quality brush is it.

Types of Brushes

The homeowner needs three sizes of paint brushes: a 4-inch brush for large areas such as walls, ceilings, paneling, foundations, siding, etc. (a roller could substitute); a 2½- or 3-inch brush for shutters, windows, woodwork, stairs, shelves, beams, baseboards, gutters, down-

Parts of a good brush are shown in art and photo below. Side of brush is cut away to show how it is put together. Parts of a good paint brush are: (1) flagged tips to hold paint and flow it onto the surface smoothly; (2) thick bristles pick up paint, release it evenly and produce a flexing action; (3) spacer plugs; (4) heel locks bristles in; (5) balanced wood or plastic handle.

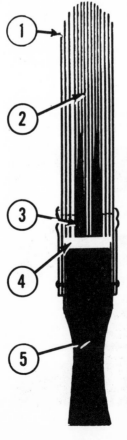

  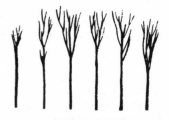

BRISTLE   **NYLON**   **EXPLODED TIP TYNEX NYLON**

Three best types of brushes have flagged ends. Hog bristles naturally flagged, others artificially.

 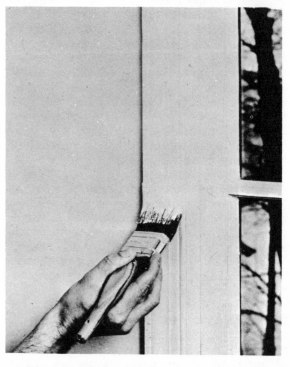

Brush should be dipped half way into paint, then tapped lightly against side of paint container.

For best control, hold brush comfortably in your hand, much like you would when holding a pencil.

Wrap brush properly to maintain its shape. Cut a piece of oilcloth or heavy paper to size shown.

Wrapper should be five times width of brush and folded as shown, keeping bristles straight, neat.

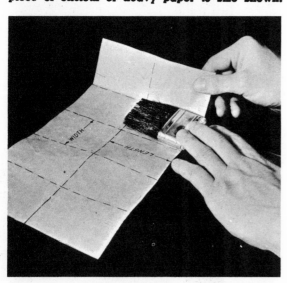 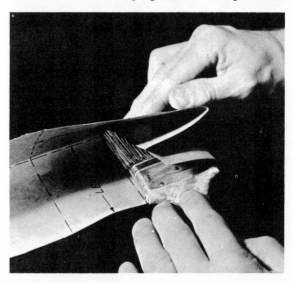

Illustrated here are some of the problems you will have with brushes due to improper care and usage.

FINGERING

FISHTAILING

CURLING

SWELLING

MATTING

spouts, board fences and the like; and a 1- or 1½-inch oval or angled sash tool for painting windows, moldings, screens and other small, detailed jobs.

Painting time will usually be saved by choosing the widest brush practical for the job. Pick an oval or round brush for rounded surfaces, a flat brush for flat ones. In painting rough surfaces use an old brush for first coats, a new one for the final.

Keep separate brushes for oil-base paints and water-thinned paints. You'll also need a special brush for clear finishes because once color gets into a brush, it affects any clear finish applied with it. Put an identifying mark on the handle.

A flat varnish brush of the fine finishing type is best for clear finishes. Undyed, unbleached natural white bristle brushes are especially good for varnish. A varnish brush has softer bristles and is chisel shaped at its tip for easier flowing and better "cutting in" on a variety of surfaces.

Natural bristle brushes need preconditioning to prevent their porous bristles from soaking up paint and becoming stiff and hard to clean. To precondition it, stand the brand new, wrapped brush upright in raw linseed oil for at least 24 hours, preferably longer. Let oil soak thoroughly into its bristles. Then remove most of the oil by drawing the brush over an edge of the container. Twirl the brush rapidly between your palms to remove more oil and wash it in turpentine to take out the rest of the oil. Remove most of the turpentine before starting to paint.

Before you actually paint with a new brush, dip it in paint and stroke it over a rough surface a dozen times or so to work out any loose bristles.

Painting

There is a knack to using a paint brush. Dip it slowly into the paint pot, letting paint penetrate half the length of the bristles. Then tap the brush lightly against the lip of the paint can. A larger, thicker brush half loaded with paint works better than a too-small brush that is fully loaded.

When painting with a brush, hold it at a 45-degree angle using the flat side from tip to midpoint of the bristle.

Always start painting at the top and work down. Avoid lap marks by painting in narrow strips less than two feet wide. Apply paint using the brush tip in short horizontal strokes. Smooth out paint with the brush empty using long strokes and light, even pressure. Wherever there is grain in the surface being painted stroke *with* the grain not across it to avoid a rippled paint surface. Always paint from an unpainted area to the painted area. Blend each brush stroke into the fresh paint.

While you paint, frequently slap both sides of the brush against an uncoated area

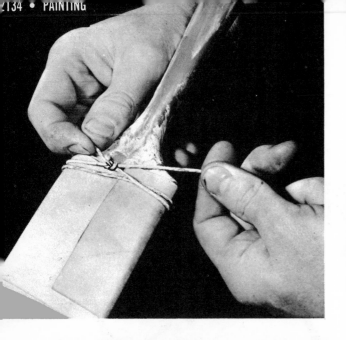

Wrapped brushes should be fastened at top with heavy cord and tied with a simple overhand knot.

Pour linseed oil into the wrapper and soak in oil for 72 hours, then wrap in newspapers to store.

Plastic ice cream tubs make good containers for the home painter. Use them to soak brushes, etc.

If caked paint in dried brush is stubborn, let soak a bit, then work well and comb out any lumps.

to release any paint that may have accumulated in the heel. Do this only when the brush's paint load has been used up. Tell the neighbors you're swatting tsetse flies.

When you take a short break, stop at the end of a board or at a door or window to avoid lap marks.

When you stop painting for a longer time, it's best to clean your brush and cover up the paint can. With fast-drying water-thinned paints you may just wrap your brush in a damp cloth and put a lid on the paint can.

Cleaning a Brush

Clean your brushes immediately after finishing a paint job. If water-thinned paint was used, flush any excess paint from the brush under a water faucet and wash the brush in warm water with a mild soap or detergent. Rinse thoroughly.

If an oil-base or other nonwater-thinned paint was used, soak your brush for several minutes in a recommended thinner for the paint. Work the thinner through the bristles with your fingers or by pushing against the container. Squeeze with your fingers to remove paint from the heel. Change solvent several times if necessary to get the brush clean. Solvent is cheaper than a new brush. If the bristles are gummed up with paint, use a wire brush or putty knife to remove it.

If the brush is to be stored, give it a bath in fresh water and rinse, working the bristles with your fingers. Shake out excess water. Then comb the bristles with a broad-tooth comb to smooth out any tangles.

Wet or dry, never let a paint brush stand on its bristles. They will soon become curled and deformed, ruining the brush.

Brushes that have become caked with paint can be made useable again with a good brush cleaner. Work a brush back and forth in cleaner, letting it penetrate thoroughly. Follow the directions on the container. When the bristles have been softened use a wire brush or brush comb to scrape out accumulated paint. Work globs of paint from the ferrule outward. Rinse again in brush cleaner. Then go through a normal cleaning as though you'd just finished painting. In cleaning synthetic-bristle brushes, stay away from solvents like alcohol or lacquer thinner. These soften nylon bristles like they soften heads.

When using a flammable brush or roller cleaner, keep away from open flames and do not smoke. Some of these cleaners are dangerous and should only be used outdoors.

Brushes that won't be used for a time should be wrapped up in aluminum foil, oilcloth or heavy kraft paper, not newspaper or anything with printing on it, and stored.

Brush Problems

Improper use and care brings brush problems:

Fingering results when the brush is used edgewise or drawn edgewise across a paint container to remove excess paint. Fingering can also be caused by soaking a brush in water. Pounding a brush, dabbing it into small corners and letting it stand on its bristles for any length of time all produce fingering.

Flaring comes from letting paint collect and harden in the heel of a brush. Proper use and cleaning will avoid it.

Shedding of bristles may result from improper cleaning methods, such as twisting or wringing a brush to remove solvents. Soon bristles break off at their setting. Shedding can come from using a brush in paints or thinners that are harmful to its bristles.

Swelling is sure to result from letting a brush rest in paint too long, causing an accumulation of paint at the heel. Clean your brushes thoroughly after every use.

Curling is caused by allowing a brush to rest in the solvent or paint can on its bristles.

Matting results from working a wide brush in narrow spots, such as a corner between two walls, so that its sides get pinched and worn. Always paint with the

To rejuvenate a paint-caked brush, use a commercial brush cleaner and work bristles thoroughly.

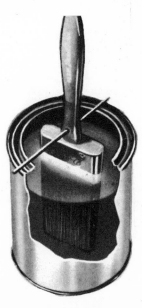

When storing an unwrapped brush in solvent or in linseed oil, suspend it by wire through handle.

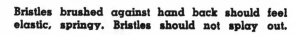

Check for good brush by exposing plugs in heel. Each should be about one-fourth heel thickness.

Look closely at the flags on the ends of brush's bristles. The more flags, the better the brush.

Bristles brushed against hand back should feel elastic, springy. Bristles should not splay out.

Twirl a new brush before you buy it to see if it will dislodge any more than just a few bristles.

flat side of a brush by angling it into corners (see illustration).

Fishtailing comes from painting pipes or narrow moldings with a wide brush. Using just the center portion of a brush is sure to cause fishtailing. To avoid it, use the proper size brush for the job.

Rollers

A paint roller is good for use on walls, ceilings, floors, rough-textured masonry and other large, flat expanses. Rollers are excellent for painting wire fences too.

Most rollers consist of four parts: wire frame, handle, cylinder (or end caps), and sleeve.

Special rollers are designed for painting pipes, wire fencing, ceilings and floors (with a long handle), corners, sash and trim.

Paint rollers are usually used with a special sloped-bottom tray. Paint is picked up by dipping the roller in the well portion of the tray, then it is evenly distributed by rolling back and forth on the tray's sloped bottom.

For big jobs a large container such as a 5-gallon pail is sometimes used. Fit the pail with a metal grid to use in distributing paint on the roller.

A roller tray's well should be about half full. A pail should be filled about one-third.

Pressure-feed paint rollers are not recommended for the average home handyman. The time-consuming clean-up just isn't worth it.

Roller Covers

The most critical part of a paint roller is its cover. Resist the temptation to buy one of the disposable roller covers. They don't work as well as the quality kind. The roller cover should be matched to both paint and job. Roller covers are available

Rollers come in a variety of naps. Shown at left, left to right, are sponge, carpet, dynel, mohair, and lambswool. Each has use.

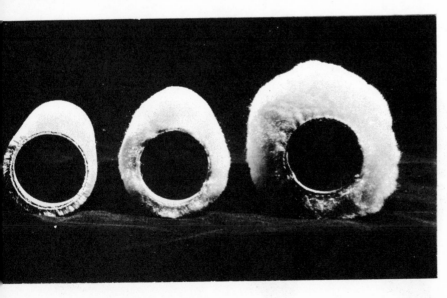

Short-nap, medium-nap and long-nap rollers also serve different purposes. Rougher the surface to be painted, longer the nap.

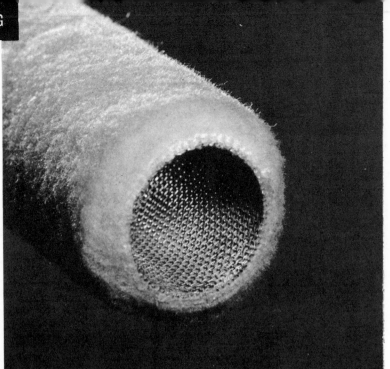

Roller cover with a wire cloth core lets cleaning solvents penetrate the cover to thoroughly clean.

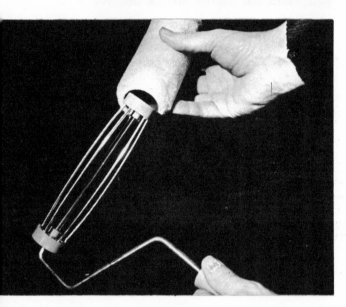

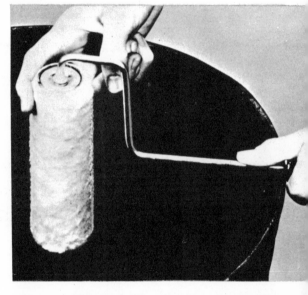

Roller cover slips on and off cylinder for fresh change of covers during job or for cleaning off.

Tool available, of course, is a shaped scraper designed to remove excess without any big mess.

When washing paint off a roller, one of the best ways to remove excess is to strip it with finger.

Take roller off to wash it. Water-thinned paint may be rinsed under the tap. A little soap helps.

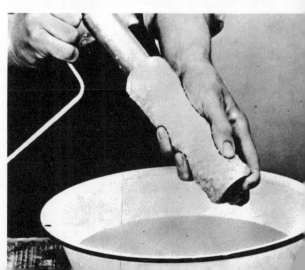

Soap up roller and rinse it under tap for getting out colors. Several rinsings may be necessary.

in short nap (¼-inch), medium-nap (⅜-inch) and long-nap (¾ to 1½-inch). Use short-nap covers for varnish, enamel, oil-base and alkyd paints on woodwork, floors, paneling and other smooth surfaces. Since a smooth, brush-like texture is produced, short-nap covers can be used in conjunction with a paint brush to do the detail painting.

Use medium-nap rollers for latex paints on all surfaces and for other paints on sand-finish plaster, concrete and masonry, textured and grained paneling and other smooth to semi-rough surfaces. These hold more paint than comparable short-nap covers.

Long-nap roller covers may be used for all types of paint on cinder block, stucco, brick, wire fence and other rough or irregular surfaces.

The smoother the surface, the shorter the nap; the rougher the surface, the longer the nap.

Select the proper roller cover material, such as:

Lambskin, which varies in nap-length from medium to long, is good with oil-base paints, portland cement paints, rust-inhibitive paints and masonry and stucco paints, not for enamels or water-thinned paints.

Plush mohair is available but you'll be better off using one of the synthetic covers (next below).

Dynel, Dacron and rayon covers are man-made fibers of short to medium nap and are good with most paints including alkyd, rubber-base, flat oil-base, casein and latex paints.

Wool is ideal for metal painting and other interior and exterior work using oil-base, rust-inhibitive and aluminum paints, but not for water-thinned paints.

Carpet is the roller cover material to use for a fine stippled finish, inside or out. A mild orange-peel stipple is created.

Use the widest practical roller for the job. A 9-inch roller is faster, while a 7-inch roller is lighter and easier to manage. For painting narrow wall areas, a 3-inch trim roller can come in handy. There are even donut-shaped rollers that will paint both sides of a corner at once.

Good rollers cost a lot less than good paint brushes, but—as with brushes—there are varying qualities of rollers. If you want long trouble-free operation, get the best. The better rollers are designed to make it easy to change covers, even in the middle of a job.

Begin rolling in a corner and work out. Start by making a large W to get good paint distribution. On vertical surfaces the first stroke should be upward even if the general direction of the painting is down. Continue by rolling in several different directions with a zig-zag stroke for even coverage. Use a moderate, even pressure. Finish each load by rolling on one direction and lifting the roller at the end of every pass. Don't lift quickly or, as much fun as it may be, spin the roller at the end of the stroke, however. Avoid the tendency to roll out the paint too thin, particularly if you are using a one-coat paint. Most short-nap covers will coat 4 to 6 square feet on a single dip. Medium-nap covers will do 10 to 12 square feet per dip.

Roll slowly. Rolling too fast causes

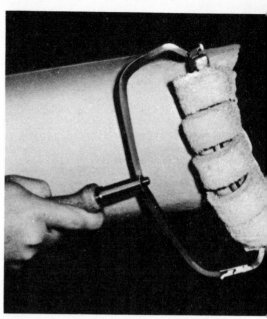

Special roller mounted on a flexible shaft, above, makes it easy to roll paint onto round pipes and large ducts.

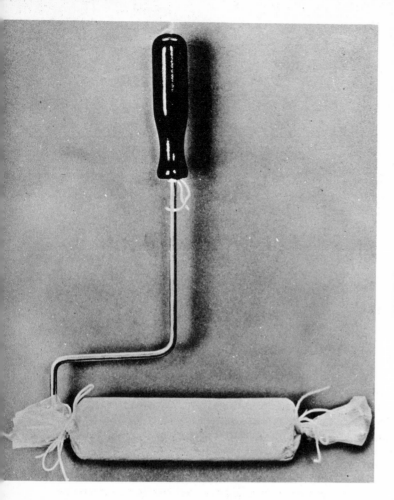

Store a cleaned roller by wrapping it in plastic, tying up the ends and hanging it up; at left.

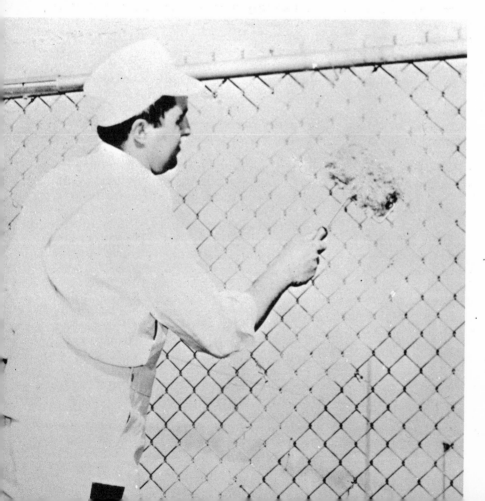

Roller with long lambswool nap cover makes quick work of painting wire fencing. One pass on each side does the job.

A roller with a long handle is handy for use on floors, ceilings and on outdoor slabs as shown here.

misting, in which fine droplets of paint settle out all over you and wherever else you least want them.

A sponge pad coater is handy for painting into corners. Pads are made in many sizes to give a razor-sharp edge and duplicate a roller's texture.

Stir paint in the can before filling your roller tray from it. If the paint thickens, thin it back to normal consistency with recommended solvent.

Roller Clean-Up

Cleaning a roller is easy if you do it right after you're through painting. First, run the roller around on newspapers to remove all excess paint. Then pour a little of the proper solvent in your tray and clean both tray and roller cover with it. Take the cleaned cover off and wash it out in warm water with a detergent. Long-nap rollers may be combed to straighten the fibers. Wipe the cover and put it aside to air-dry. The roller frame and end caps or cylinder can be cleaned with a solvent-dampened cloth. Put the roller parts where they'll be ready for the next use. Roller trays are easier to clean if they are lined with aluminum foil before use.

Besides brushes, rollers and sponge pads, a large lambswool mitt is useful for painting things like pipes and downspouts. Coverage is good and clean-up is not too tough.

Light colored walls and ceiling push back the walls and raise the roof imparting a spacious feeling.

How to Use Color

The basis of all color is light—so herein we shed some light on color. . .

LET'S FACE IT . . . color is the really fun part of painting. Nothing gives you a bigger lift than seeing that luscious clean swath of color peeling from your roller or brush to cover dull old walls or weathered siding. Great—but will you love it in December as you did in May? You will if you choose the paint with a background of understanding what color is, how other conditions affect color, how it affects surroundings and viewers and how you can make it work for you.

Sound like a waste of time? Consider the time and money wasted when the "bargain" kitchen paint makes Mom nauseous. Or imagine the traumatic results of chosen-on-a-lunch-hour house paint that makes a home the most outstanding in the neighborhood. Outstanding like a sore thumb. To have more fun with color there are some things you should know.

Just for openers here are a few basic terms so you can speak the language like a native.

Color and *hue* are used interchangeably. *Tints* result from adding white to colors. *Tones* are made by adding gray to colors. *Shades* are produced by adding black to colors.

Value refers to the lightness or darkness of a color. Tints are light-value colors (or high-key), shades are dark-value colors (or low-key).

Intensity refers to a color's purity. The 12 pure colors of the standard color wheel (Fig. 1) are the most vibrant of colors and have the greatest visual impact.

To be scientific, color is what you see when light reflects from a surface to your eyes. Objects themselves don't *have* color —they absorb some of the sun's rays and

Paint a giant of a house elephant gray and watch it shrink. Light-colored entry adds good accent.

reflect the ones we see. Therefore, the basis of all color is light, specifically sunlight. Sunlight consists of six colors—violet, blue, green, yellow, orange, red. These have almost unlimited combinations and are used to make all the colors that we surround ourselves with.

Digressing from the scientific, black, white and gray may not really be colors but, with artistic license, they are considered neutral colors by decorators. As such, they can be placed in any color scheme without changing it. Wood tones are usually treated as neutral colors too.

The Color Wheel

A workable palette of colors has been devised, which includes the six colors of sunlight and six others. Known as pure hues—full strength colors—these comprise the standard color wheel. Red, blue and yellow, the *primary* colors, are equidistant around the circumference of the color wheel. By mixing equal amounts of the adjacent primary colors, purple, green and orange result. These are *secondary* colors. The other spaces on the wheel are filled by the *tertiary* colors, again, equal combinations of adjacent colors. These are red-purple, red-orange, yellow-orange, yellow-green, blue-green and blue-purple.

Because we've long associated them with fire and the sun, reds and yellows give an instant feeling of warmth. These colors, red through yellow-green on the color wheel, are grouped as *warm* colors. The *cool* colors are those of the sea and sky:

blue-green through purple. Green and red-purple have enough of both qualities in them to fit into either category. They're called *intermediate* colors.

Color Harmony

Get a good grip on that standard color wheel because it puts *you* in the driver's seat. See what it can do. Experiment and experience have worked out a set of guides for using color in pleasing combinations. This is called color harmony by the cats who know:

Monochromatic harmony is the simplest of all color schemes (Fig. 2). Only one color is used, varying it merely by grading the value into several tints, tones and shades. At best, monochromatic harmony is restful, dignified and unifying. At worst, it is monotonous and dull. A monochromatic color scheme is best suited to small rooms.

Analagous harmony (Fig. 3) involves colors that are next to each other on the color wheel. Usually three to five colors are used. Mother Nature chose this harmony in painting aspen leaves yellow-green, oak leaves green and setting them against blue-green spruce trees. Analagous harmonies are soft and subtle, useful for creating overall warm or overall cool effects.

Complementary harmony (Fig. 4) makes use of the sharp contrast of colors directly opposite each other on the color wheel. Vivid, dramatic, gay, it can also become monotonous. Color complements are a

STANDARD COLOR WHEEL

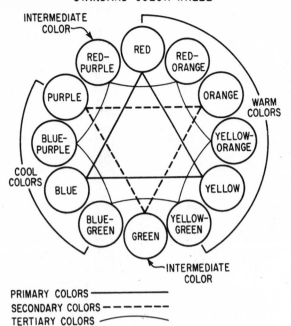

PRIMARY COLORS ————————
SECONDARY COLORS — — — — — —
TERTIARY COLORS ⌒⌒⌒⌒⌒

Fig. 1—Study this diagram—get to understand.

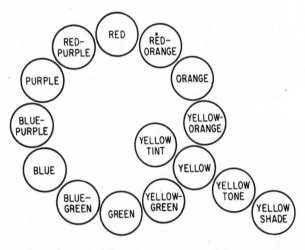

Fig. 2—Monochromatic harmony, using one color.

Fig. 3—Analogous harmony—using related group.

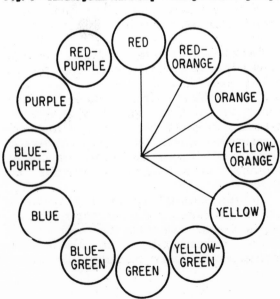

good choice for children's rooms, play and activity areas. Combined with black and white for visual variety, they can be used in other living areas of the home as well.

Split-complementary harmony (Fig. 5) adds the richness of a third color to a complementary color scheme by using the basic color and the two flanking colors of its direct complement. Split-complementary is a popular color scheme.

Adjacent-complementary harmony (Fig. 6) is a variation of true complements that adds a color from either side of one of the complements.

Double-complementary harmony (Fig. 7) gives four colors to work with by carrying split-complements one step further. That is, use of the two colors on either side of directly opposite colors.

Mutual-complementary harmony (Fig. 8) combines analogous and complementary systems. Choosing five adjoining colors from the wheel, the complement of the central color is added. A further step, *split-mutual complements* (Fig. 9) uses the colors on either side of the complement, for a total of seven colors. However, color combinations of more than 3 or 4 colors should be used only in large rooms.

Triad harmony (Fig. 10) is another popular pattern. Using three colors equally distant on the color wheel, it can be varied in numerous ways by choosing pure hues, tints, tones or shades of the principal colors.

With the color harmony guides to go by, choosing a color scheme is almost mechanical. One factor is left to you, however, that of *proportion*. Keep in mind that all color schemes (except monochromatic and analogous harmonies that are used for special effects) should include both warm and cool colors—but not in equal amounts. Similarly, a color scheme should avoid the use of opposite colors in equal amounts, as well as equal amounts of light-dark combinations. These acts of chromatic fence-straddling create confusion and uneasiness in a room. Stay off the fence.

Another aspect of proportion covers the number of colors. Three to four is par for the average room. To avoid a busy look, any more than that calls for a proportionately larger area.

In spite of what has been said about the purely mechanical ease of choosing a home color scheme, YOU must be satisfied with the colors. If they don't please you, then no amount of "rightness" will save them. Don't permit colors you do not like.

Color linkage is a term decorators use when referring to the flow of color from

A large, bulky house looks smaller when painted a dark color. Contrasting accents confine attention.

Dark roof and deep toned paint on second floor lower square house. Dark doors lengthen and accent.

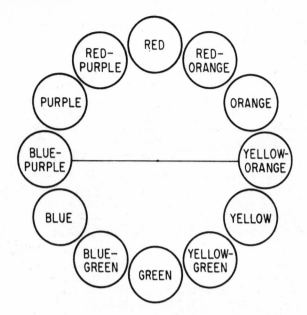

Fig. 4—Basic complementary harmony. Opposites.

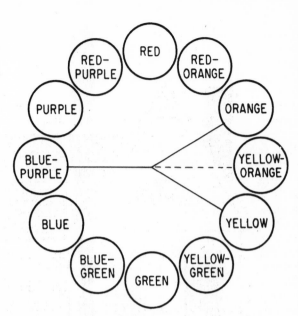

Fig. 5—Split complementary harmony. Interesting.

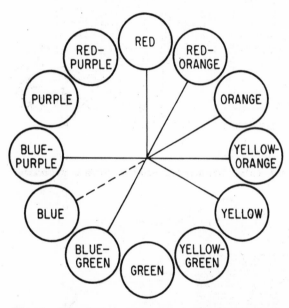

Fig. 6—Adjacent-complementary harmony. Tricky.

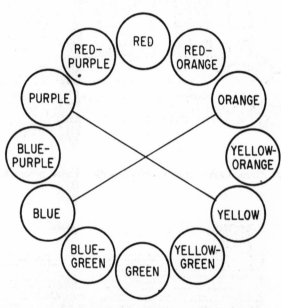

Fig. 7—Double-complementary harmony. Perfect.

one room to another. Today the pro's, and those of us who would emulate them, treat a house as a whole color unit. Rooms are often open to one another. Because of this there should be a traceable repetition of key colors throughout—sometimes as principal colors, sometimes as accents. For swinging results include the exterior house colors in your overall planning. (More about that later.)

Color Illusion

The hues of the color wheel can do more for your decor, though, than fall into pleas-

ing combinations. They can create the illusion of architectural changes, alter the apparent sun-exposure of a room, establish the emotional mood of a setting. These qualities can be summed up as *color illusion*. Keep in mind these basic ground rules of color illusion—they're good problem-solvers.

Warm colors—advance or come toward the viewer visually, thus tending to make objects look larger, rooms smaller. They create intimate settings. Warm colors *look* warm and are stimulating, cheerful.

Cool colors—recede or back off from the

viewer visually, thereby making rooms look larger and more spacious. They *look* cool and are quiet, restful.

Light colors—expand because they reflect light, thereby making rooms seem more spacious and objects seem larger yet lighter in weight. They not only look cooler, they actually *are* cooler because they reflect light. Light colors are cheerful and tend to switch you on.

Dark colors contract because they absorb light, thus making objects appear smaller yet heavier in weight and rooms look smaller and more confining. They not only look warmer, they actually *are* warmer because they absorb light. Dark colors tend to sit on you. Used in excess, they can be depressing.

Bright colors (high intensity)—expand because of their eye-catching color purity, thereby exaggerating the size of objects and causing areas to close in visually. They are stimulating, gay and can be distracting or unrestful when used in excess.

Outside Color

Color on the outside of your house shouldn't be just a matter of "white because it's customary." Neither should paint sale bargains nor personal preference alone make the choice. The exterior color scheme of your house should please you and your family and give a happy feeling that "this is my pad." Moreover, it should work for you in four different ways: (1) give the maximum value from your home's design; (2) help establish a house's own distinctive character; (3) blend your house harmoniously with its surroundings—both natural and neighborly; (4) make use of color magic to help correct architectural faults.

Is your home an early American or Dutch colonial style? Emphasize the distinctive projecting second story by painting it a different color from the lower story. If your home features a covered walkway or handsome entry, these should be accented with brighter colors than the body of the house.

The long, low lines of a rambling ranch-type house can be emphasized by horizontal color accents. If the house has high windows such as in bedroom and utility areas, use the lower edge of these as a horizontal line projected the length of the house. Paint upper walls a different color.

Multilevel homes will look the part if one section is painted a different color, provided the color is carried over to adjacent sections to link the whole as a unit.

Climate should affect color choice too. Warm sunny climes are best for pastels and

Enlarge small window and door openings with built-up trim, moldings, plus a sharp light accent color.

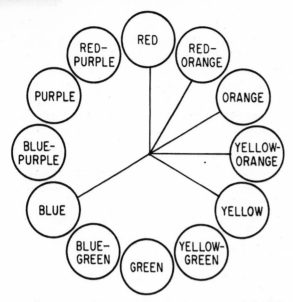

Fig. 8—Mutual-complementary harmony. Colorful.

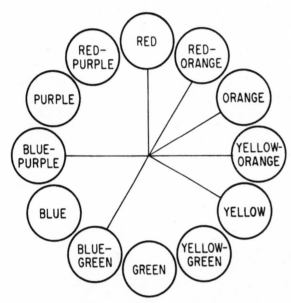

Fig. 9—Split and mutual-complementary harmony.

Fig. 10—Triad harmony. Balance tones carefully.

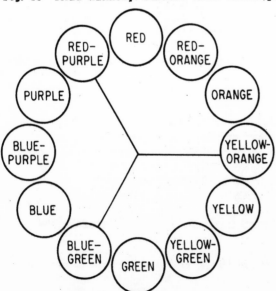

vivid colors that would be in jarring contrast to the grayer skies of other climates. The latter take best to grayed tones.

Then you have to consider the immediate setting of your house. Is it surrounded by trees, set in an expanse of green lawn? Or do neighboring houses provide its framework? What looks great with emerald green may clash with brick red. To a lesser extent your home should be considered in relation to the neighborhood, to your own block. Should you yearn to stand apart from the crowd in a big way, give second thoughts to a future of being "Smith, you know, the cat in the lurid lavender house."

Save the lavender for your boudoir and feel *secretly* superior. It's easier on the family, the neighbors and your home's resale value.

Outside Color Styling Tips

Here's a hatful of hints to keep in mind when color styling the outside of your home:

Color illusion works outside as well as inside. Review the rules.

White or a light roof best reflect the sun's rays and keeps your home cooler in summer. Avoid the dark colors except in the case of a real architectural problem.

Very dark colors near the foundation line keep foundation plantings from showing to advantage.

Don't outline your house with accent colors, or give it the measles by accenting every bit of trim.

Fence or garden walls can pick up accent colors and tie the house into its setting.

Once the outside of your home has established its own individual character, pick up the color cues and move indoors. Entries and rooms with large glass areas should utilize the principal exterior color or colors to give an easy transition from outdoors to indoors with no abrupt breaks.

Not many people can start interior decorating from scratch. For those with unlimited color choice, the main guidelines are personal preference, suitability to environment and, in the case of just-marrieds, adaptability to future decorating expansion.

Using the color wheel makes color harmony almost automatic. Starting with any color that appeals to you, you can work out combinations until you hit one that grabs you. Even within the chosen pattern there's room for adjustment by shifting emphasis from one color to another.

House of many materials can be unified by painting the whole in two tones of the same basic color.

Minimize confusion of added dormers, etc., by painting them same color as roof or dark tone of trim.

In addition to the color wheel, you can use a painting, a rug or yard goods for a color guide. Starting from scratch or redecorating, this is a neat trick. If you have furnishings to reckon with, building a color scheme from a yard goods print may be your best bet. Unwanted furniture colors can be slipcovered to conform.

But whether you spin the color wheel or take your color cue from a dime store Rembrandt, remember to test your selections in the actual physical surroundings of your home. Six years, the life of the average interior paint job, is a long time to live with the wrong color.

Let the picture portfolio clue you in on the can-do's of color. If you have a problem room or house to paint, review the rules of color illusion and get set. Paint problems??? Color them solved! •

Universal tinting colors (also in cans) are available in many colors and may be used in most paints.

How to Mix Your Own

There will be those times when this information can be very useful indeed.

SO WHAT if everyone agrees that ready-mixed paints are much better. So what if thousands of different colors are available in ready-mixed paints. So what if most paint merchants now have color-mixing machines and can custom-mix a paint right in the store accurate to 1/32nd ounce of colorant. And so what if the mixing of colors takes a good eye and no small amount of know-how.

The need to create a color of your own may be overwhelming and you'll want to do it anyway. It might be a faded living room paint that needs touching up in spots. It might be a wallpaper color that you want to pick up and carry to an entire room. It might even be that you bought some paint on sale and want to change its color. Whatever it is, the task of mixing your own colors is not impossible. Just color it difficult.

Since it would take too much space to cover all about color-mixing of paints, only the high points can be hit.

If you possibly can, get your dealer to do the mixing and matching for you. Take him a sample of the color you want and leave it with him. This will give him time to do a good job. Some paint-wallpaper dealers have had so much practice in handling colors that they have become quite adept at it. Some dealers offer this as a special service to customers. Enjoy, enjoy.

If you mix your own, there are two ways to go: (1) use tinting colors from tubes, or (2) mix colored paints.

Mixing colors from paints is all right if you have the right colors and they're all of the same brand and same line within that

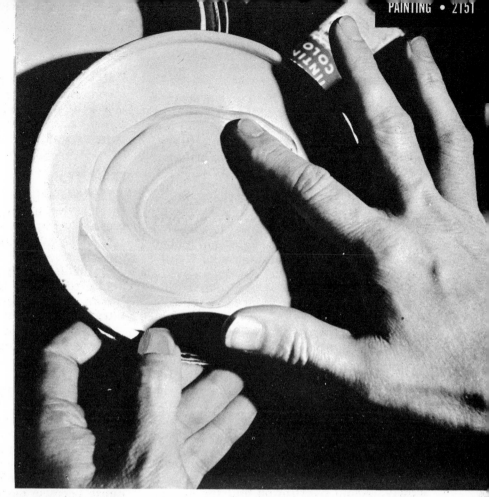

Test a small amount of tinting color on the paint can lid to see what the effect will be. Doesn't work? No sweat. Try again.

To aid in blending in a tinting color mix it with a little of the paint. The top of a used-up aerosol can is a handy bowl.

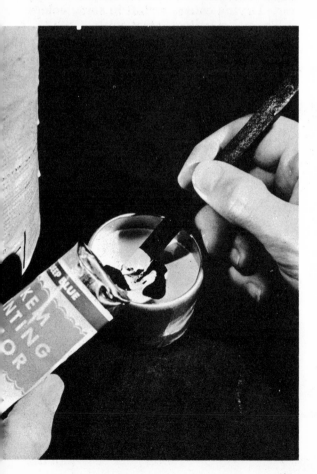

brand. But don't try to combine two or more unlike paints. You may end up with a mixture that has some serious flaw, perhaps one that makes it wrinkle up on drying.

The better way to mix your own colors is to use tinting colors, the kind in tubes that are available in a wide range of hues. Added to white or to ready-mixed colored paint, tinting colors are squooshy for easier mixing. The most convenient kind are the universal colorants. These may be used in water- or solvent-thinned paints, for flat, semigloss and gloss finishes indoors and out. Many manufacturers of universal tinting colors don't recommend them for adding to lacquers.

A 1½-ounce tube of tinting color costs about 60 cents. Besides tubes, they're sold in half-pints and quarts.

For best results usually no more than 4 ounces of tinting color should be used per gallon of paint, although some manufacturers approve more. Check the label. Starting with white, it is impossible to produce a very deep color with only four ounces of tint per gallon. If you're after a dark color, you'll have to begin with one that's close.

The Tinting Colors

All of the tinting colors have a predominant hue (pure color) with overtones of another hue. Analyze the color to be matched for its basic hue—red, blue, green, yellow, etc.—with each tinting color being used.

Ask yourself, what is its basic hue? What overtones of other hues are peeking out at you? What tinting color does the tone make when added to white? It helps to study the manufacturer's color-chip folder, which often shows various amounts of tinting color added to white.

The tinting strength of the color is important, too. Some have more strength than others.

Add tinting color to the base color slowly, checking the value after thorough mixing.

Mixing in a tinting color is easy if you go about it right. Mix enough paint for the whole job. Pour a small amount of the paint into a separate container and add the tinting color to it. Stir thoroughly. Add the mixture to the original container and stir until the color is uniform.

Since there is a tendency to underestimate the strength of tinting colors, proceed slowly. Avoid overtinting and the subsequent need for adding base paint to tone down the mixture.

Remember that almost any color (1) is a combination of several hues (2) is usually a tint of these hues and (3) it has been toned. Try to separate these various components and add tinting color to the base paint to supply the missing ingredients.

Good Tips

Nothing will take the place of experience in color mixing but there are some basic truths that apply to all paints:

1. Black cannot be made. Dark gray, but not black.

2. Brilliant reds and browns cannot be made from white bases. Start with red or brown and add other reds or browns or pure hues, *but not white.*

3. Choose a base paint in a lighter shade than the color being aimed for. It is always easier to darken a color than to lighten one.

4. When mixing, always mix the tint (adding white), then the tone (adding black in order to gray the color). Reversing the procedure can be difficult.

5. In color matching, start with the basic hue and gradually add the overtone colors. Dry a sample before arriving at a color depth because most paints deepen on drying. Drying causes a shift in some colors.

To make yellow, start with a white, a

Stir the tint into large can thoroughly, working paint up from bottom and off sides of the container.

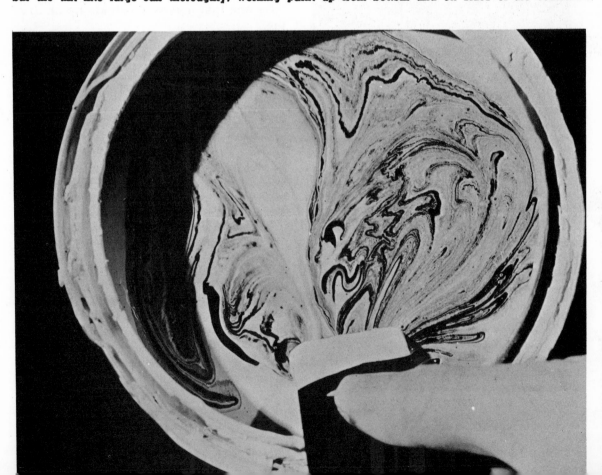

Approach a color match slowly. When you get close, let a sample dry. Some paints change upon drying.

lighter yellow or a clear ivory base and add yellow tinting colors.

To make blue, add tinting colors to a white base.

To make red, begin with ready-mixed red paint and add the tinting colors needed to reach your goal.

Very deep greens can be made with hansa yellow and lampblack. The yellow changes the blue in the black to green.

Browns are made from burnt sienna or burnt umber with the addition of enough sienna and black to overcome the red overcast in the burnt sienna or burnt umber.

Beiges are "in" now. Have been for some time. They are tints of brown and can have yellow, sienna, red and even green overcasts. Beige paint can be made from green by adding fast red or American vermilion. Beige can be made from blue or aqua by adding hansa yellow and fast red. Beige is made from yellow or ivory by adding burnt sienna and chrome green D. In fact, almost any color except gray can be made into beige.

Gray is made from lampblack (blue gray) and raw umber (warm gray). Almost any color can be made into gray by adding its complement.

Use a minimum number of tinting colors, especially with latex paints. Using strongly contrasting tinting colors may produce color differences at overlaps, etc., when the paint is applied.

Finally, be sure that you use either a water-dispersible or universal tinting color for latex paints.

TINTING COLORS

Hansa Yellow—A brilliant yellow with greenish overtones. Excellent for clear, light tones of yellow. A strong color.

Lampblack—A blue black that makes blue gray. With yellow, make olive tones. A strong color.

Yellow Oxide—A raw sienna color. Beige with slight red overtones. Makes cream. Of medium tinting strength.

Thalo Green—A brilliant green with decided blue overtones. Excellent for clear, light tones of aqua. A strong color.

Red Iron Oxide—A burnt sienna color; reddish brown; decided earth color. Good for soft pink. Of medium tinting strength.

Chrome Yellow Medium—A creamy yellow. Sienna overtones. Makes creams and golds. A strong color.

Fast Red—A brilliant red with violet overtones. A strong color.

Brown Iron Oxide—A brown color with red overtones. Excellent for beiges. Medium tinting strength.

Calbizol Violet—A brilliant violet with decided blue overtones. A strong color.

Chromium Oxide—A dull green making tones of green. Low tinting strength.

Raw Umber—A warm gray brown with gray overtones. Of medium tinting strength.

Thalo Blue—A brilliant blue of excellent permanence. Produces clear tints. A strong color.

Molybdate Orange—A sharp bright orange. Clear tints. A strong color. •

Elegant Clear Finishes

The steps are sanding, bleaching, staining, filling and finish coating.

GETTING a really fine finish on interior woodwork, paneling and floors is so different from ordinary house painting that it rates special treatment. It's no sweat to produce admirable clear finishes that will last for years.

There are five steps to building an elegant clear finish: sanding, bleaching, staining, filling and finish coating. Not all of the steps are used on every job.

If there is one secret to getting an elegant clear finish, it's surface preparation. A surface should be made as smooth as possible before applying any finishing materials. If the wood already has a clear finish that is sound, you can sand and recoat with the

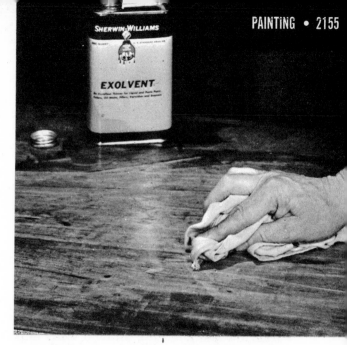

Prestain, if possible, working on horizontal and wipe with a lint-free cloth after stain has set.

To darken, recoat and wipe again. To lighten a stain that has dried, wipe with turps or solvent.

A final waxing will give clear-finished paneling, such as this western pine, an added protective coating and bring out sheen.

Photo at left shows the panels being prestained before installation. The stain is applied with a brush, wiped when it sets.

same or a compatible clear finish. Otherwise begin with bare wood.

Bleaching

Bleaches can be used to lighten the natural color of a wood, to make the color of new wood more uniform, or to modernize old dark-stained woodwork by lightening the stain. There are several types: One is made by dissolving oxalic acid crystals in very hot water. Common household bleach can be used straight from the jug for wood bleaching. The most effective wood bleaches of all, though, are made specifically for the purpose and consist of two solutions that are mixed just before use.

Bleach is applied with a synthetic rubber sponge. Wear rubber gloves. And if you forget, only your doctor will know for sure.

When the bleached surface is dry, go over it gently with a damp cloth or sponge to remove any residue. Another bleach application may be necessary to get the result you are after.

Allow 12 hours of drying and then sand thoroughly to cut down the wood grain raised by bleaching.

Sanding

Whether wood has been bleached or not, careful, thorough sanding is the most important step to a really fine finish. Do all sanding with the grain using the proper grade of abrasive.

If you tackle anything as extensive as a paneling or floor finishing job, latch on to a power sander. A belt or pad sander can be rented or purchased. A big job sander for floors is easy to get from most of the tool rental cats.

For sanding of wood choose aluminum oxide or garnet paper. Flint paper is bad news except for throw-away use. Forget it.

Hardwoods can be sanded initially with 3/0 paper (also designated *120 grit* and *fine*). Sand softwoods initially with 2/0 paper (*100 grit, fine*) and this is as fine as you need to go for an average finish. When abrasive paper gets dull, throw it away and take a new piece.

In floor sanding begin with No. 2 or No. 2½ paper, sanding across the grain or at a 45 degree angle to it. On a second sanding use a finer No. 1 or No. ½ with the grain. Finish up by sanding with the grain using No. 0 or No. 00. Pick up all sanding dust with a vacuum cleaner.

For the very best wood finish, dampen the wood all over with a warm, wet cloth to raise the grain so it can be evened off later by sanding. Allow the surface to dry overnight. Sand lightly with 6/0 or 8/0 (*280 grit, extra fine*) paper. If a water stain is to be used, prewetting is necessary to keep the stain from causing any grain-raising of its own. The water treatment also brings up any small dents for a smoother surface.

Fill any nail holes, cracks, gouges or other indentations with wood putty that matches the color of the wood. Let the wood putty harden, then sand surface so that it is smooth all over.

Staining Wood

Staining eliminates the raw look of certain woods and can make plain woods look like more exotic ones. Stain can also make woods blend with other colors in the room. Stain can enhance the beauty of nicely grained wood—witness mahogany with a fine piano-type finish.

Stains are made in both oil and water base. The advantage of an oil stain is that it doesn't raise the grain of the wood being stained. Stains of the same type may be intermixed for special effects.

Some stains may be tinted to produce interesting effects. The result should be tested on a scrap of the wood, though. If no sample is at hand, test on an inconspicuous portion of the wood to be finished. Remember that stain on a small piece of wood

Like paneling, trim is easiest to finish if it is done before installation. Work on newspapers.

looks lighter than it will on a large expanse of paneling.

The result of any staining job depends to an extent on the amount of wiping that is done after the stain has been applied. For this reason it's a good idea to try the stain-and-wiping process on a sample of the wood. When you are satisfied with the effect, proceed with the whole project.

Apply stain to one section at a time using a brush or lint-free cloth pad. When the stain begins to lose its wet look, wipe off any excess, shading the appearance as you go. Allow it to dry overnight and sand lightly. Dust with a tack rag.

Adding an extender to oil stain will do away with the wiping operation. Sherwin-

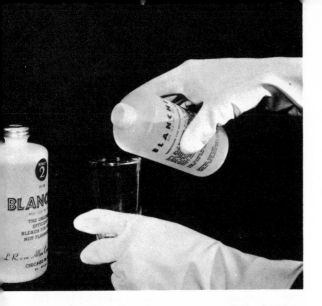

For bleaching, mix the amount needed of a two-part bleach in a clean jar. Wear rubber gloves.

Apply bleach to the wood using a sponge. When dry, sponge off with water to remove any residue.

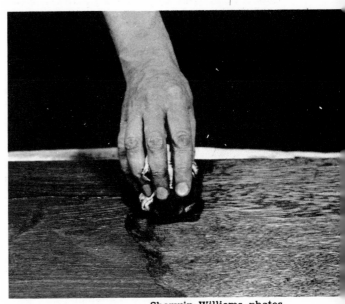

Sherwin-Williams photos

Apply wood paste liberally, working it well into the pores of the wood to smooth out coarse grain.

Wipe off excess across the grain with a circular motion. Finish with soft cloth with the grain.

Williams makes one called *S-W Oil Stain Non-Wipe Extender*.

If stain sets in a wood too long and becomes too dark, it can be lightened by wiping with turpentine. Allow overnight drying.

Filling

Wood filler is like a finishing school for wood. Some woods require filling in order to smooth a coarse grain texture. Those that do are oak, mahogany and walnut. Birch, maple and gum have such small pores that they don't usually need filling. The softwoods, such as fir, redwood, pine and cedar never need filling. If a wood's grain texture is not objectionable, you're home free on filling. Just don't count on a finish coat bridging over grain. It won't.

To hide coarse grain apply paste wood filler. This is a heavy-bodied material that needs to be stirred well before using. To ready it for use, reduce the filler with either turpentine or other thinner called for on the label. Aim for about the consistency of melted ice cream. For filling dark-stained woods, reduce wood filler with an oil stain of the right color to keep filled pores from showing as light spots in a dark surface.

To use paste wood filler, apply it to the thoroughly sanded surface. Brush on liberally, working it well into the wood pores. When the filler begins to "flatten," as they call it, or lose its wet look, wipe off the excess with a rough-textured rag. Burlap will do fine. Use a circular motion and pat filler into the pores as you go.

Wipe off any filler that's still left with a clean, soft cloth, wiping across the grain of the wood to keep from wiping out any filler. Finish by a light cleanup wiping *with* the grain. Let filler dry overnight, sand it lightly and clean the surface with a tack rag.

Once wood filler hardens it is tough to wipe from the surface. Therefore, cover only an area that you can conveniently wipe in time. A cloth moistened with turpentine or solvent will help to soften any wood filler that becomes a problem. Sand with 6/0 or 8/0 paper.

Sealing

Some woods—notably fir plywood—have such a wild grain they require sealing of the bare wood. One quick-drying sealer is shellac. If a really natural wood finish is wanted, don't use shellac. Even white shellac darkens wood. Lacquer-type clear sealers change a wood's appearance the least.

One of the combination sealing stains may be just the thing. Many are fast-drying allowing you to complete the operation quickly and go on to the next step. You can even make your own sealing stain by mixing oil stain with a nonpenetrating sealer, the heavy-bodied type containing nonhiding pigments that preserve the natural appearance.

Clear Finish

Choosing a clear finish for wood depends upon what effect you want and how much time and money you are willing to put into it. The chart of clear finishing systems is based purely on the author's experiences and should be taken merely as neighborly advice. Your other neighbors might not agree.

The easiest and richest truly clear wood finishing system I have used consists of one coat of lacquer sanding sealer smoothed with 6/0 paper and followed by two or three coats of clear lacquer. The final coat can be glossy or satin, depending on the surface wanted.

I have found that the best natural finish, where slight yellowing is permissible, is two coats of Satin *Behr-Lac* made by Behr Process Company. This clear interior fin-

CLEAR FINISHING SYSTEMS

SURFACE	RECOMMENDED FINISH	PREPARATION AND FINISHING	EXCEPTIONS AND ALTERNATES
Cheaper panelings, doors, woodwork, trim	Satin Behrlac	Sand, seal if necessary, stain if desired and give two coats, steel-wool-scuffed between to remove dust specks.	For no discoloration of blonde woods use clear lacquer or polyurethane.
Exotic paneling where a deep, rich finish is desired	Satin clear lacquer	Sand, seal if necessary, stain if desired, fill if needed and sand, apply clear lacquer sanding sealer, sand and give three coats clear lacquer.	Can use polyurethane coating sanded between coats, but not over lacquer sanding sealer.
Floors	Polyurethane, moisture-cured type	Sand, patch nail holes, fill if necessary, stain if desired and give two coats not more than 24 hours between.	Can use other type of polyurethanes, but moisture-cured type is hardest.

A handy sanding block can be made by cementing felt to wood and wrapping sandpaper around it.

Folding sandpaper into four thicknesses enables it to work well into crevices and molding grooves.

A belt sander is ideal for finishing paneling. The easiest way is to sand the paneling on a flat surface before you start installation work.

ish brushes on and dries quickly without brush marks or excessive dust-catching. It's not as clear a finish as lacquer, but it is hard wearing and does not peel or water-spot. My wood-paneled house, including exposed wood plank-and-beam ceilings, has been finished with this product. Some has aged ten years and is still like new. I'm sold on *Behr-Lac*. (Honest, no connection with the manufacturer or anything shady like that.)

The hardest-wearing clear, nonyellowing finish I've found is polyurethane. Two or three coats resists just about everything. This recently developed finish outlasts varnish on floors, can be brushed or sprayed and dries quickly without dust-collecting.

Some handymen lean toward varnish for a clear finish. Others feel there's no clear finish quite like shellac. (Could it be the alky in it?) Clear finishes are available in semigloss and glossy. While woodwork can be made glossy if you like, large wall expanses such as paneling should not be so shiny. There are two ways to achieve non-

glossy clear-finished surface: Use the kind of clear finish that dries to a satiny luster. Or hand-rub a glossy finish with pumice and oil or extremely fine abrasive paper after it has been dried.

For a finish that is *in* the wood not on it, apply either Danish oil or one of the stain-wax finishes. The use of Danish oil involves a good deal of hand-polishing to get a fine finish. Stain-wax produces a hand-rubbed effect simply and economically. It does not change the wood's appearance because the wood isn't covered up. Stain-wax combines all the essential ingredients of finishing in one product and no staining or sealing is necessary. The material is made in a number of tones. Consult the label for directions.

Special effects can be created on clear-finished wood by making the grain one color and the rest of the wood another.

Once you get a clear finish on woodwork or paneling, you'll probably want to wax it. Not only will wax provide protection, it will make dusting easier too.

Painting Concrete and Masonry

Use the right paint, make sure the surface is clean and go to work.

MASONRY SURFACES, such as cast concrete, concrete blocks, brick, stucco and cement-asbestos are sometimes painted to make them more decorative. Unlike wood, though, masonry does not ordinarily need paint to protect it.

Painting concrete and masonry is just as easy as painting wood—maybe easier—but there are a few catches to look out for. The chief one is alkali. All masonry surfaces contain alkali . . . from the cement. New ones contain the most. After a time the surface alkali content diminishes but some is still left no matter how old the masonry is. The solution is to coat masonry only with paints that have built-in resistance to alkali. Select from among the several types of alkali-resistant paints according to the kind of service they must give. Let a thorough reading of the paint container's label be your final guide to selection.

Latex

The three common latex paints—polyvinyl acetate, acrylic and styrene-butadiene—are excellent for most masonry uses. If the job is outdoors use the polyvinyl acetate or acrylic types. All three types may be used indoors. While these paints have a damp-proofing effect, they form a film that permits the masonry structure to breathe. Blistering is practically eliminated. And since latex house paints are compatible with water, the masonry need not be perfectly dry. Instead it should be dampened just before applying the first coat to keep thirsty pores in the masonry from soaking up your $6-a-gallon paint before it can harden into a film.

Latex house paints are self-priming. They may be used directly on concrete and masonry, even on new surfaces. They may also be applied over old painted masonry if the old paint is in good shape. But because latex paints cannot penetrate chalky surfaces enough to cling tightly to them, a sealer-coater should be used over moderately chalked old paint. The alkyd polyvinyl-acetate-type sealer-coater is simplest to use. Dampen the surface before applying it.

As ideal as they are for masonry, none but the latex floor paint is abrasion-resistant enough to be used on floors, walks, swimming pools and the like.

Painted masonry can make the structure of a house blend or contrast with the rest of its features.

Rolling paint on concrete is much like painting a wall. Roll out excess on hardware cloth in can.

To stain a concrete slab, pour penetrating stain onto the cleaned surface. Have the spreader ready.

Use broom, brush or roller to spread stain. Use second application later if richer color wanted.

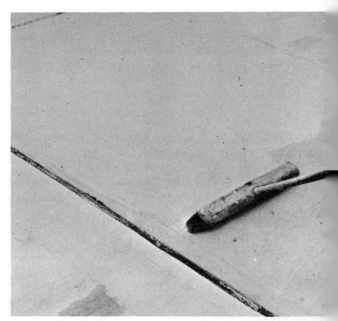

Pittsburgh Plate Glass photos

CONCRETE AND MASONRY PAINTING SYSTEMS

LOCATION	RECOMMENDED PAINT	SURFACE PREPARATION	APPLICATION	EXCEPTIONS AND ALTERNATES
Outside concrete and masonry walls and stucco	Latex paint, exterior	Fill any porous surfaces with grout and prime. Dampen well before first coat.	Self-primer Two coats Brush, roller or spray	Oil-base stucco and masonry paint can be used for damp-proofing on well-aged surfaces. Portland cement paint is best on very rough or moist surfaces.
Inside concrete and masonry	Latex paint	Fill any porous surfaces with grout and prime. Dampen well before first coat.	Self-primer Two coats Brush, roller or spray	Portland cement paint is good for basement walls, if preferred.
Cinder or slag block walls	Chlorinated rubber to guard against staining	Get surface clean and free of dust.	Self-primer Two coats Brush, roller or spray	Portland cement paint may be used.
Floors, decks, porches, patios, walks, swimming pools	Chlorinated rubber floor and deck paint	Etch new or glossy floors with 10 percent solution of muriatic acid.	Self-primer Two coats Brush, roller or spray	For heavy wear use catalytic coatings. Portland cement paint may be used on pools.

Alkyd

While alkyd paint is often recommended for painting masonry, it lacks good alkali resistance. However, some manufacturers claim to produce alkyds that are good on masonry. Use them if you are convinced they're better than latex.

Chlorinated Rubber

Not only does chlorinated rubber paint provide excellent alkali resistance, it can be made to be highly resistant to water penetration and abrasion. For these reasons chlorinated rubber floor and deck paint may be applied to sidewalks, patios and the like. Special chlorinated rubber swimming pool paint may be used on pools. Chlorinated rubber paint can be used indoors too if you wish. It is made in a wide range of colors. This self-priming paint adheres well either to new masonry surfaces or to chalky surfaces left by old paint. Use this type of paint over cinder or slag block walls to keep stains from showing through, as they might with a latex paint.

Portland Cement Paint

Made strictly for painting concrete and masonry, portland cement paint is a mixture of white portland cement, lime, a coloring agent and, in some, finely ground sand. Cement paint is particular about where it is applied. It must be used either over bare masonry that is in good condition or over previously applied cement paint. It possesses little or no adhesion to surfaces that have been coated with other types of paints.

Portland cement paint is purchased as a dry powder and mixed with water before using. Setting is by hydration of the portland cement, just as with concrete.

Portland cement paint has a history of success in painting masonry. Alkaline itself is not subject to attack by alkali. It is applied by brushing with a stiff bristle brush and does a good job of sealing the surface against the entry of large quantities of water. Cement paint clings tenaciously, even to continually moist masonry surfaces. Cement paint is fine for filling small cracks and holes in porous masonry. For this use get Class B paint that contains sand to act as a filler. Class A cement paint contains no fillers and is used where the surface texture is to be preserved.

One coat of portland cement paint is usually enough for interior walls where weathertightness is not a factor. Surface texture as well as sound absorption values are better preserved when one instead of two coats of paint is used.

Portland cement paint is at its best in white and light colors. Dark colors tend

Clean wall thoroughly before painting it with portland cement paint. Fill cracks with mortar.

Walls must be bare masonry or previously painted with cement paint. Dampen wall but do not soak.

Mix portland cement paint in clean container to consistency of thick cream. Follow directions.

Use a potato masher or piece of hardware cloth to pulverize lumps, get mixture smoothly blended.

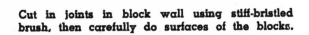

Cut in joints in block wall using stiff-bristled brush, then carefully do surfaces of the blocks.

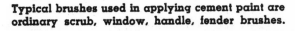

Typical brushes used in applying cement paint are ordinary scrub, window, handle, fender brushes.

to be uneven. Cement paints make an excellent base for other paints of any color. Since cement paints are not as easy to apply as the newer coatings, their best use is probably for painting in moist locations where water resistance is needed. Portland cement paints may be used indoors or out. They have little abrasion resistance, however, and should not be used on floors or other surfaces that are apt to get wear. Find some other paint for your dragstrip.

Painting should be done when the temperature is sure to stay above 40 degrees F. for at least 12 hours. New masonry should cure a month before painting with cement paint.

Since cement paints will not stick to glossy troweled-smooth surfaces, these surfaces should be etched first with a 10 percent solution of muriatic acid. To make it add one part muriatic acid out of the jug to ten parts water in a clean plastic or enamel container. Whenever you work with strong acids wear rubber gloves, goggles and protective clothing. Always dampen masonry before scrubbing it with acid. This will prevent the acid from being absorbed deeply into the masonry where it may do substantial damage. Flush all acid off completely with clear water before painting.

Catalytic Coatings

Great strides have been made in catalytic coatings in the past few years. Two types of these hard-wearing coatings are available: those with an epoxy-ester base and the two-package types, which contain vegetable oils, such as linseed, soya, castor, etc., to react with the epoxy resin.

Epoxy-ester-base coatings may be clear or pigmented. They come in gloss, semi-gloss and flat finishes.

Two-package epoxies, which are often referred to as "tile-like coatings," are combinations of epoxies and polyamide resins. When the two components are mixed, the resulting paint may be used like any other paint. However, it usually sets up in about eight hours and must either be applied before that time or discarded.

Catalytic coatings possess the ability to cling tightly to most surfaces—not just masonry—have excellent chemical resistance and great abrasion resistance. While they will protect against weather, these coatings are not very resistant to weathering. They lose their gloss easily when exposed to sun and rain. If lasting gloss is wanted, don't use epoxies outdoors.

Catalytic coatings give good service on concrete block, concrete walls and floors, swimming pools, garage floors and walls, and laundry floors and walls. Colors are varied. Their big drawback is a high price. For this reason, the use of a catalytic coating is best limited to locations where other less expensive coatings will not work. Possibly their best uses are for painting swimming pools and for holding back water that is stubbornly trying to seep through porous or cracked basement walls.

Catalytic coatings can be applied directly to masonry but never over old paint. Follow directions on the label for application.

Oil-Base Stucco and Masonry Paint

Similar to conventional oil-base house paint, oil-base stucco and masonry paint is usually reinforced with special resins that somewhat improve its alkali resistance. Application is like oil-base house paint. Oil-base masonry paint is usually made in a low or flat sheen that tends to hide surface irregularities.

If you are determined to use oil-base paint on masonry, have a good reason. Here are two of them: (1) oil-base paint provides greater dampproofing than latex paint and (2) it simplifies painting masonry and adjacent wood trim to get a matching effect. Some manufacturers claim there are others.

Surfaces for oil-painting should be clean and dust-free. Oil-base paint should never be used on new masonry surfaces without pretreating them. Some experts even recommend treating weathered masonry too. Treatment consists of washing with a 10 percent solution of either muriatic acid or zinc chloride in water to kill the alkali. After rinsing and drying thoroughly, two coats of oil-base paint are usually applied with several days' drying time between coats.

Block Filler

Block filler is designed for filling the texture and small cracks in concrete and cinder blocks. It's a water-thinned preparatory coating that provides a smoother and more uniform surface on which to apply exterior and interior finishes—except portland cement and catalytic coatings. Made in white, block filler can be tinted if desired. It's not worth a darn on surfaces that have been treated with silicone water repellent.

Surface Preparation

No matter what type of paint or coating you apply to concrete and masonry, the surface must be clean. Use a wire brush

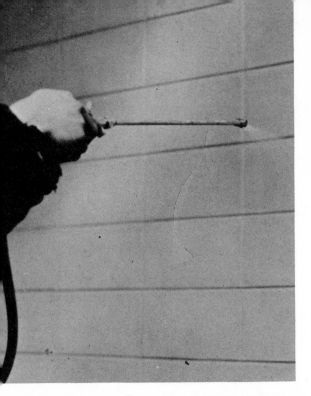

After painting with portland cement paint, fog-spray to keep wall damp for 2 or 3 days afterward.

A long-nap roller is a good way to paint rough-textured masonry. Long fibers reach in to cover.

to remove all dirt, loose particles and anything else that might interfere with paint adhesion.

Remove all grease and oil from the surface by washing with trisodium phosphate (TSP) and hot water. Cast concrete or precast concrete, such as cement-asbestos shingles, may have a wax or form-release agent on the surface. Get rid of this by washing with a cutting solvent like benzine or by several months to a year of weathering before painting over it. Because benzine is highly flammable, weathering is the safest method if you have the time.

A white salt-like substance on masonry is probably not salt but efflorescence. Caused by the leaching of dissolved salts to the surface, most efflorescence can be removed by dry-brushing. If this doesn't work try scrubbing the dampened wall with a 5 to 10 percent solution of muriatic acid and rinsing after the bubbling has stopped. Before an acid treatment is used on any wall, the acid should be tested on a small, inconspicuous portion to be certain there is no bad effect.

After dirt, grease, oil and efflorescence have been removed, wash or hose the surface to complete the cleaning job. Let it dry before painting unless a water-thinned

paint or cement paint is to be used. Then painting should be done while the surface is still damp.

If the surface has been painted before and the paint is in good condition, use a wire brush to remove loose materials like dirt. Old paint that is loose, peeling or heavily chalked must be taken off before repainting.

When a water-thinned paint is to be used on concrete containing metallic objects such as nails and steel form ties, these should be spot-primed with a good anti-corrosive metal primer before painting proceeds.

Of course, if a masonry surface is broken or soft and crumbling, looking like it was mixed in a martini glass, it must be repaired before you can paint it successfully. Chip out the deteriorated material down to solid concrete. Brush a creamy portland cement-and-water grout on the surfaces to be repaired, then patch them with a workable, plastic 1:3 cement-sand mortar. Treat the freshly cured patch as new concrete when painting over it.

Paint may be applied to masonry by brush, roller or spray. The two main points to remember are: (1) use the right paint and (2) have the surface clean. •

This peeling paint job will require removal down to bare wood. Painting over would only peel again.

How to Get Paint Off

When necessary, old paint can be removed with chemicals, heat or abrasion.

PUTTING PAINT ON can be a great pleasure; getting paint off is a drag. Avoid it if you possibly can. But, if an old paint has some incurable defect, is built up too thick or you want to change from one type of paint to another and the two are not compatible, you may have no choice but to remove an old paint film.

There are three ways to do it: chemical, heat and abrasion. Chemicals are applied and let stand long enough to soften the paint film so that you can scrape it off down to bare wood or metal underneath. Heating works the same way. Paint is abraded off by sanding.

Chemical removal may cost more than heat removal but it's faster. There's a drawback, though. Some paint removing chemicals leave a caustic residue that has to be cleaned up before repainting can proceed. Because sanding stirs up a lot of dust, it isn't very satisfactory indoors unless you use the type of sander that catches its own dust. Sanding cannot be completely avoided, however. When paint is removed

chemically or by heating, the surfaces still need some sanding. There's no clear-cut choice as to the one best method. Use the one that seems the least obnoxious.

Chemical Removers

Chemical paint removers are made in liquid and semipaste forms. The liquids work best on horizontal surfaces, while the pasty ones are best for vertical surfaces.

The better chemical removers contain methylene chloride plus other solvents such as alcohols, acetone and benzol. While methylene chloride adds to cost, it boosts paint-removing ability. Methylene chloride also makes a remover less flammable.

One nonflammable type of paint remover contains a strong caustic.

Because of the powerful solvents and strong caustics that removers contain, it's a good idea to keep from getting paint remover on your skin or in your eyes.

Apply paint remover as thick as you can get it using a full-haired brush. Lay the remover on with the flat side of the brush in one direction only and follow the manufacturer's instructions as to how much area to coat at one time. As soon as the paint has been softened sufficiently by the remover (test with your fingernail), take the film off with a scraper. Thickly built up paint surfaces may need two or three coats of remover. You can either recoat without scraping or scrape off what paint will come loose and then recoat with more remover to take off the rest of the paint.

At times it helps to scour the softened paint with steel wool to further loosen it before scraping.

Some removers require washing with water to remove their residue before repainting. Others contain wax to slow the evaporation of their solvents and keep them wet longer. Wax must be taken off with a solvent such as turpentine or benzene before painting again. Still other removers need only cleaning with #1 or #2

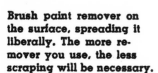
Brush paint remover on the surface, spreading it liberally. The more remover you use, the less scraping will be necessary.

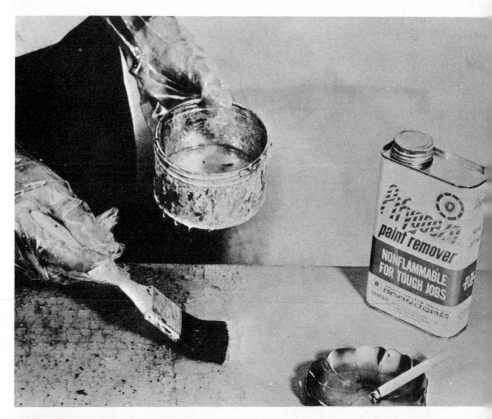

When chemical remover has softened paint, scrape it off as completely as you can. What's left may need another application.

Give yourself a hand. Always wear protective gloves when working with paint remover. Keep the stuff out of your eyes.

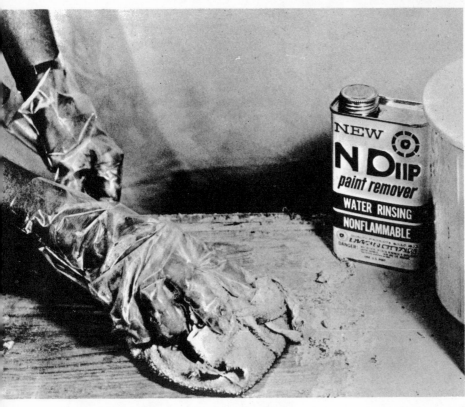

Thoroughly clean up the residue left by the paint remover with a turpentine-soaked rag. Follow manufacturer's instructions.

steel wool and a chance to dry for four hours or so before they're ready for a new coat of paint. (See the manufacturer's directions.)

Treat a chemically cleaned surface as new wood or metal when repainting.

The prime caution when using flammable paint removers is to avoid fire. Some removers are highly volatile with low ignition temperatures. When you get a gallon of something as burnable as this spread out on your wall or floor, there is considerable danger of fire. For this reason, it's a good idea to avoid use of the extremely flammable removers. Ask your dealer.

In general it takes about a gallon of paint remover to cover 200 square feet of surface. A gallon costs from $4 to $6 or more, depending on the ingredients.

Heat Removal

For burning paint off you will need one of three tools: a blow torch, a propane torch or an electrically heated paint removing tool.

Actually, in removing paint with heat,

Semi-paste removers are best for clinging to vertical surfaces where the liquids would tend to run off and fail to work.

paint is not really burned off the wall but merely softened so that it can be scraped away more easily. *Less hardly* might be a better way of putting it.

When using a torch to remove paint, aim it onto the surface at an oblique angle and keep the flame moving to avoid setting the paint on fire. If you are right-handed, work from right to left. As soon as the paint softens behind the torch, scrape it off with a long-handled scraper that is designed for use with heat. The long handle keeps your hands away from the flame. Wipe the scraper off occasionally and keep watch for smoldering areas. If the paint should flame, the torch is either being held too close or being held in one spot too long.

Use the flame removal method outdoors only when there is little wind. Keep away from open windows with flying curtains. Be careful with the fire bit if you don't want your house to end up a fully mortaged pile of rubble. Also keep the flame from heating window panes. It might break the glass.

Electric paint removers contain a heating element that glows cherry red and a reflector that concentrates heat at the surface. And what seems like a 1000-foot cord connects them with the nearest electrical outlet. The higher their wattage the faster electric paint removers will work. They're operated much like a torch but should be moved in a slow pass over the paint, slow enough to leave it softened ready for scraping. A scraper with a bent blade is often used.

Burning paint off is especially good for removing thick coats that would eat up lots of chemical paint remover. It is fine, too, for getting off polyurethane and epoxy coatings that laugh back at some of the chemical removers.

After burning paint off, the surface should be sanded to clean it up for repainting.

Sand Paint Off

If you choose the sanding method of paint removal don't try to do the job by hand. Use a power sander. For any sizable area, hand-sanding is just too much work.

The best sander for removing paint is the belt sander. It cuts out material fast and sands in a straight line with the grain to leave the wood ready for repainting. A belt sander that is to be used for much paint removal indoors should have an attachment for collecting dust. This can be either the type with a built-in vacuum system and dustbag or with an opening for attaching a household vacuum cleaner hose.

While a disc sander removes material fast, too, there are some drawbacks to using one. There is no way of collecting the dust.

And unless you're a born winner at controlling it, the discs will gouge circular grooves in your wood. These are sure to show in the final finish. Also, discs have a nasty tendency to get caught between cracks in boards and go sailing off. Great fun, but you can go through more discs that way. If you disc off paint, you'll have to finish up with some other kind of sander to sand out circular marks left by the disc.

While it is slow at paint removal, an orbital sander may be used particularly for thin build-ups of paint. The kind that converts to straight-line action for fine finishing is best.

No matter what sander you use, choose an open-coat abrasive paper for removing paint. This will last the longest before it becomes clogged. Use 60-grit for fast paint removal, 80-grit for a finer job. Whenever you're not sure which grit to use, always start with the finer paper and switch to the coarser one if progress is too slow. (It usually is.)

Keep a power sander moving in order to avoid digging into the wood in any one spot.

Paint left in out-of-the-way corners after power-sanding will have to be removed by hand using a wood sanding block to back up a piece of abrasive paper. These spots can be scraped free of paint if you prefer.

Scrapers

Knife-type wall scrapers for removing paint are made in sizes from 1¼ to 6 inches wide in both flexible and stiff blades. Usually the 2- to 4-inch-wide scraper with stiff blade works best. A putty knife can be used if it is stiff enough.

Other types of scrapers have curved blades for scraping contours.

For the final clean-down a wood-han-

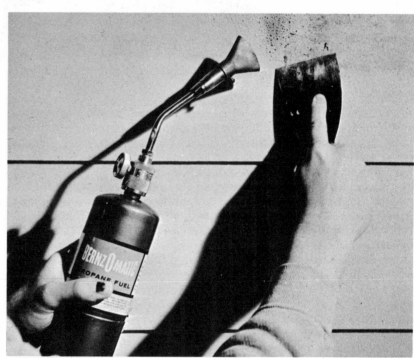

To burn paint off, heat an area until the paint softens, then scrape off. Keep torch moving, avoid scorching the surface.

This electrically heated paint remover has a built-in scraper that lifts off heat-softened paint as tool is moved forward.

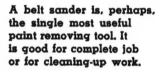

A belt sander is, perhaps, the single most useful paint removing tool. It is good for complete job or for cleaning-up work.

dled scraper with hooked blade is useful. These can also be used for scraping off loose or peeling paint even without the aid of a chemical remover.

Paint Removal Tips

When using paint remover indoors on walls and ceilings, cover electrical outlets with masking tape. Take off all hardware, such as door knobs, handles, etc. Carry a pail around with you to catch paint scrapings. These contain solvents that are harmful to any painted surface they touch. Don't let them drop onto a painted or varnished floor or (it couldn't happen to a nicer guy) you'll end up refinishing that, too. Protect it with newspapers instead.

Using a large, flexible scraper on plaster and plasterboard wall surfaces will help you to keep from gouging into the wall.

Paneled doors and other fancy-work contain crevices that not only resist scraping but the paint may well be thicker there than on flat surfaces. Go at these with a small scraper blade or with a wire brush. Use additional remover on them and clean with coarse steel wool and a wire brush. Scrape fancy moldings with a special tool,

or file the corners of an old putty knife rounded so they will fit into the crevices of these moldings.

Don't try to treat too large an area with chemical remover, especially if there is much detail. The remover may dry out before you get all the paint scraped off.

Either get furniture out of the room or cover it with a dropcloth.

If possible, take doors off and lay them across two sawhorses to remove paint from them. Chemical paint removing is always easier on horizontal surfaces because the remover can be flowed on thicker.

To remove the finish from floors, first do a two-foot-wide area across one end of the room. Take up the softened paint and put the sludge in an old can. Then work on the next area

In business or in stripping paint from stairs, it's easiest to start at the top. Work on several stairs at once.

No matter how you approach it, paint removing is no picnic. Scraping and sanding off paint is hard, dirty, messy and unsatisfying work. Who needs it? Keep smiling, though, roll with the punches and you'll soon be done.

Painting Ideas

Whether decorating, detailing or defining, paint is readily applicable.

SO FAR this book has shown plenty of the why and how of house painting but not much of the what. Here is *what* . . . what some others have done with paints.

If you see anything that grabs you, feel free to use it next time you paint. A good idea and a little paint can really make a lot of difference. •

Horizontally placed textured plywood panels painted in nonchalking exterior paint unify large house.

Opaque stains used on siding, wood screens and benches, deck stains on deck, exterior latex on roof overhang, chlorinated rubber in pool.

The dark brown trim paint used on the accent bricks was carried to shutters and diamond design on door. Note white steppingstones.

House in middle is made to look larger and brighter with same color exterior latex paint on both bricks and siding.

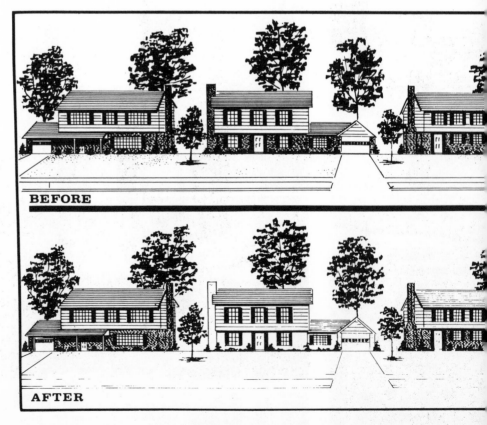

BEFORE

AFTER

Incised lines to form the diamonds in this citron-painted stucco end panel are painted brown. Rest of house is painted white.

Contrasting black-and-white shutters add interest to all-white house. The shutters are made by nailing trim over plywood.

Dark brown furnishings add accent to beige latex on textured concrete end wall. Stains make dissimilar woods used match up.

Dark-painted walls with light and white accents turn large room into cozy conversational setting.

A dramatic window shade treatment balances the contrast between modern and antique furnishings in this family room. The walls and ceilings are flat latex, furniture was antiqued from a kit.

Country yellow provincial color glaze kit was the kit used on furniture. Walls, shutters were painted.

Bright wallpaper on an end wall lent one of its colors to other walls, another one to the ceiling.

Floor was varnished, shutters sprayed, Mediterranean furniture was aged in "olé red" kit glaze.
Martin-Senour photos

Unusual geometric rug, table are complemented by painted furniture and walls, mixture in decor.
Magee Carpet photo

Special-Purpose Paints

Just knowing that these paints are available will make chores easier.

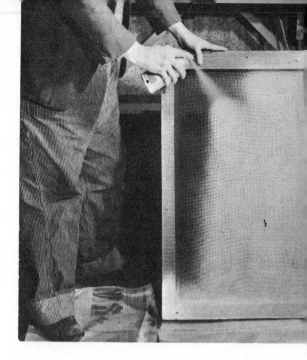

IN ADDITION to all the usual paints for around the house, there are a number of special-purpose ones. Your need for them will not be frequent or great, yet they are worth knowing about just in case.

Luminous paint—Available in small containers or aerosols, luminous paint is great for painting objects you want to be able to see in the dark. Things like switch plates, clock hands, door escutcheons and other such small items. The cost of a small amount, however, takes luminous paint out of the big-job class. Used outdoors, luminous paint needs a clear finish over it for protection.

Wood-graining kit—Usually a two-paint outfit, a wood-graining kit is useful for painting a wood-like grain on metal or almost any other surface. It may be used for creating more exotic-looking wood grains on cheaper woods, such as fir or pine. Apply the base coat and let it dry. Then apply the top coat and "grain" it with a brush or steel wool pad. The tools you need are supplied. Kits are available in woods like oak, maple and walnut. While it takes skill to do a realistic job of graining, when inspected closely, from a little distance away homemade wood is tough to tell from the real thing. The newly formed surface should be protected with a clear finish.

Antiquing kit—Similar to a wood-graining kit, an antiquing kit includes two paints —base and glaze. You can put an antique finish over furniture, cabinets, doors, walls, picture frames, anything made of wood, metal, plastic or masonry. Finishes are available in greens, beiges, browns and blues. All but the necessary clear finish is provided.

Fire-retardant paint—This paint is formulated with pigments and vehicles that dry so they will not support combustion. Furthermore, some of them actually "cook" into a film that protects against fire. Use them where their additional cost and their more difficult application would put your mind at ease.

Heat-resistant paint—The old stovepipe enamel was a heat-resistant paint available in black. Today other colors are made as well. Use them on the outsides of heaters and trash burners, the insides of ovens and the like.

Flat white—Not much used any more, flat white was once recommended as a primer and undercoat. It's still available if you want it, but should not be used as a finish coat.

Flat black—This finish is made for use on iron grillework. It dries to a dead flat black, resembling real wrought iron. Use it on iron-work of all kinds—things like lawn furniture, stair railings, etc. It comes in spray cans as well as in the regular form. Spray can is handy for touch-ups.

Multicolor enamel—This paint contains two or more colors all emulsified together in small globs. When sprayed onto a surface, they spatter it with the various colors. Multicolored paints can be used on walls, woodwork and any other indoor use you care to put them to.

Wrinkle paint—Available in spray cans, put a wrinkle paint on and it soon draws up into an aged-looking film. If the paint on your car did it, you'd be sick.

Screen enamel—Thinned-out paint, screen enamel is designed to flow around the wires in screening and coat them with-

Aerosol method is perfectly suited to painting some few screens. Spray through several.

Mask and paint switch plates with luminous paint and you'll find them in the dark.

Old world antique finish is possible with simple color glaze kit. No removal of old finish needed.

The finished product. Piece is first painted a base color, darker glaze is applied, wiped off.

out bridging across the mesh and filling it up. Screen enamel is best applied with a carpet-like applicator, or spray.

Roof coatings—There are several different kinds of roof coatings. Many can be had in black or aluminum. They are used chiefly for protecting and maintaining built-up roofs.

Fibered asphalt comes as a liquid suitable for brush, roller or spray application. Its fibers impart durability and sag-resistance. Also made is a nonfibered type that is thinner in viscosity primarily for use as a roof topping.

Asphalt emulsion roof coating contains fine bituminous particles suspended in water. This type can be thinned with water to a certain extent. It can be applied with brush or spray.

Colored aluminum roof coating includes a variety of pigments in combination with an aluminum pigmented roof coating. The vehicle may be asphalt, resinous binders or butyl rubber. Application is by brush or spray.

None of the roof coatings—or any other coating, for that matter—is suitable to waterproof a foundation, even though they are often recommended for this use. Save your money.

Blacktop sealer—Spread this on your drying out asphalt driveway and it will look like new again. Blacktop sealer is said to prevent erosion of the asphalt driveway's binder.

Lawn tint—Yes, there's even a paint (more of a stain, actually) for your grass. Spray it over the lawn, and grass will green up as though it were a fresh spring planting. ●

Wood tone kit transforms secondhand furniture into elegant mellowness with painted base coat, glaze-then-wipe second coat. Excellent results.

Pine knots bleeding through a builder's one-coat paint job. Proper sealing and painting is needed.

Painting Defects

How to prevent and correct some common, usually exterior, paint problems.

A NUMBER OF THINGS can go wrong with a paint job, nearly all of them connected with exterior painting. Don't be discouraged, though. If you buy quality paint and follow the manufacturer's directions, the chance of a defect spoiling your paint job is small.

The source of a paint problem is usually one of the following:

1. Poor painting techniques. Failure to follow the label instructions for mixing, priming and application.

2. Lack of moisture protection for exterior walls.

3. Use of the wrong type of paint for the surface or exposure.

4. Use of inferior paint.

Here are most of the painting defects, how to prevent them and what to do if your house comes down with one of them.

Blisters

There are two major kinds of blisters: temperature blisters and moisture blisters.

Each has a different cause. All blisters are bubble-like swellings in the paint. Temperature blisters don't contain water, as moisture blisters often do.

Moisture blisters are probably the most common of all paint defects. Moisture vapor inside a house tries real hard to find its way out through the walls. Often it can't and it bumps smack up against the paint film. If the vapor pressure is great enough, the paint film can be forced away from its bond with the wood. The result—blisters. Most moisture blisters contain water, either when they form or soon afterward. Pop some to see. If blistering gets bad enough, the paint will probably peel off.

Moisture that causes blistering may be generated within a house by washing, cooking, humidifying, breathing, etc., or it may originate outside the house and seep in through improperly protected exterior walls. Find where the water is coming from, if you can, and eliminate it.

A bad case of peeling like this, no matter what the cause, calls for removal of the paint down to bare wood. Subsequent coats on top would only peel off.

Temperature blisters may form when hot sun or sharp rise in temperature hits your last coat of fresh paint. Liquid thinners are warmed, turn to gas vapor.

Blistering from moisture can occur on either interior or exterior walls. Best way to combat this is to use a blister-resistant paint like latex.

An excellent guide to locating the source of blister-causing moisture in house walls appears in *Research Note FPL-0125 Blistering and Peeling of Exterior Paints Caused by Moisture,* by the Forest Products Laboratory, Forest Service, U.S. Department of Agriculture, Madison, Wisconsin 53705.

Use a blister-resistant paint—a latex will do fine—next time you paint. All the old paint will have to be removed, however, because if you leave it on, it will keep the latex paint from breathing to prevent further blisters.

Temperature blisters are different from moisture blisters. They show up within a few hours or at most one or two days after painting. They form only in the last coat of paint. They're usually caused by pressure when liquid paint thinners in fresh paint are warmed and turned to vapor. A fast rise in temperature, as when the sun's rays fall on a newly painted surface, and *zowie,* you've got temperature blisters.

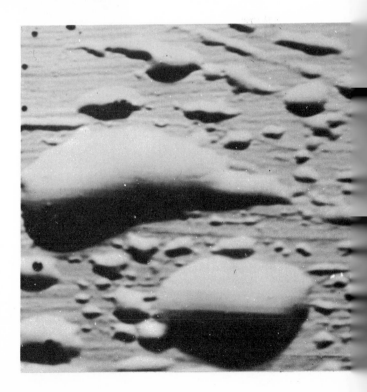

To prevent temperature blisters, follow the sun around your house as you paint. Paint the north side in the morning, east side late in the morning, south side well after noon and west side late in the afternoon.

In cold weather when your paint is thick, brush it out as thin as possible.

If you get temperature blisters, let the paint dry a few days and scrape them off. Smooth their edges with sandpaper and spot-paint the area.

Inter-coat Peeling

Inter-coat peeling is the flaking off of paint between coats rather than down to bare wood as with peeling that comes from blistering. It usually involves only the last coat of paint. The cause is inadequate cleaning and failure to get the natural degradation products of paint off protected surfaces such as porch ceilings, eaves, etc.

To prevent inter-coat peeling make sure the primer and top coat are compatible. Wash or thoroughly sand protected areas to remove gloss and degradation products. Often, paint in these areas doesn't need recoating, just washing.

If you've already suffered inter-coat peeling, the paint layer that is peeling must be removed, the surface well cleaned and repainted.

Chalking

Quality paints wear gradually so that excess chalking does not form. Heavy chalking indicates a poor quality paint or one

All blisters are bubble-like swellings in the paint. Temperature blisters do not contain water as the moisture blisters often do. Pop some to check this.

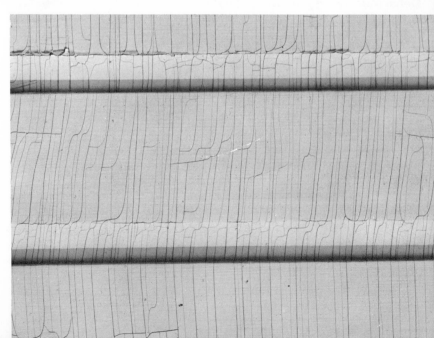

Paints that are not elastic enough to withstand constant expansion and contraction of wood due to temperature and moisture changes will crack.

that was improperly applied. Maybe both.

To correct a bad case of chalking, brush off the chalk and apply two coats of a high quality paint. If you use latex paint, the first coat should be a primer that will bond with the heavily chalked surface.

Fading

Some paints fade because the colored pigments actually change on exposure to sunlight. Old paint films may appear faded because of chalking. Fading of paint is a quality problem. Cheap colored paints fade faster than good ones. Wind-driven rain, salt air and bright sunshine all speed up fading.

As trite as it sounds, the solution to most fading is to buy quality paints from a reputable dealer. That's good advice any time.

Flaking is a pecularity of metal painting, especially common in paint applied over galvanized metal. Read text for special priming treatment.

Inter-coat peeling is the flaking off of paint between coats rather than down to bare wood. Clean off peeling paint, clean surface well and repaint.

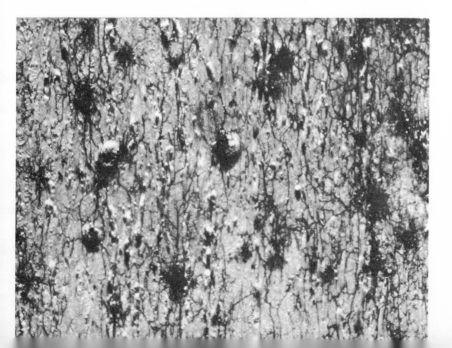

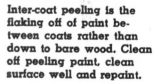

Mildew appears as dark spots with lighter areas spreading below. Prevent by using a mildewcide in paint. See text for solution used to kill mildew.

Bleeding

Painted redwood and cedar are sometimes discolored by bleeding. This happens when water gets into wood and leaches the natural colors to the surface. Proper sealing and thorough painting will prevent bleeding.

To stop bleeding, apply one coat of shake and shingle paint or exterior clear finish to keep water out. Bleeding from knots in the wood can be stopped by sanding them clean, applying a knot sealer (the vinyl butyral type is best outdoors) and repainting to match. For best results, let wood dry out before treatment.

Mildew

Mildew appears as dark spots with lighter colored areas spreading below it. These fungus stains that grow on painted surfaces and discolor them may be prevented by using a zinc-oxide-containing paint or in severe cases a paint containing mildew inhibitor. A mildewcide or fungicide can be added to paint to do the same thing. Follow the manufacturer's directions on how much to add.

To get rid of mildew that has already formed, wash with a solution of ⅔ cup trisodium phosphate (for example *Soilax*), ⅓ cup detergent (*Tide*), 1 quart household

Fungus and mildew stains that grow on painted surfaces can be prevented by using a zinc-oxide paint.

Alligatoring comes from putting hard-drying paint coat over an excessively soft one. Don't paint over pitch or tar. Always use compatible paints.

bleach (*Clorox*) in about 3 quarts warm water to make 1 gallon. Wear rubber gloves when using this solution and protect shrubs and plants from being splashed by it. Where mildew is heavy, repeated washing may be necessary.

Dirt Collecting

House paints sometimes collect dirt, usually in the form of wind-blown dust, industrial smoke and plant pollen. While house paints tend most to collect dirt during what is called their "soiling stage," later during their "chalking stage" this dirt is supposed to be sloughed off. If it isn't, washing is the best answer.

To fight dirt collecting do your exterior painting just before or during the warm, sunny part of the year. In smoky areas use a free-chalking paint that performs well locally. Your paint dealer can probably advise you. See that roof overhangs, gutters and downspouts are arranged to keep water off the wall.

Dirt that is held on paint can be removed by washing with a mild trisodium phosphate solution. Dirt collection, however, is not a good reason for repainting.

Cracking

Paints that are not elastic enough to withstand constant expansion and contraction of the wood due to temperature and moisture changes will crack. Cracking is serious. It leads to unsightly scaling and the only remedy is complete paint removal down to bare wood. You're much better off to avoid cracking than to have to repair it.

The secret to keeping cracking away from your door is to follow good painting practices. Consider using a latex paint. To keep from getting it on too thick, follow the manufacturer's recommended spreading rate when painting. And don't repaint unweathered, protected areas such as porch ceilings unless they really need it.

Loss of Gloss and Color

When paint is thinned too much or spread too thin, much of its oil may be absorbed by the wood or previous paint, causing it to dry with less than normal gloss. If colored, the color may be faded. The problem is termed loss of gloss and color. Some areas may seem lighter than others and some may shine more than others. Sometimes the defect is even all over. Loss of gloss and color may show itself as soon as the paint dries, or it may take several weeks to develop.

To avoid loss of gloss and color, thin and

Blue stain grows in damp wood, must be kept dry. Treat with water repellent; can be bleached out.

Crawling occurs when there is a contraction of freshly spread paint on too-young or oily surface.

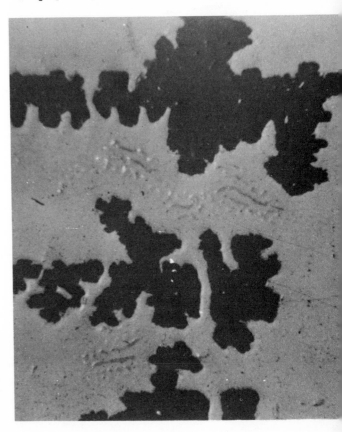

spread paint according to the manufacturer's directions. Paint when the weather is favorable.

Early loss of gloss and color can be remedied by another coat of paint. This is recommended when the defect occurs in the initial paint job on new wood. Applying another coat of paint is not recommended when the defect occurs in repainting over old paint that is in reasonably good condition. In this case there is some danger that one more coat of paint may make the total paint film thick enough to cause other, more serious, paint problems. In that case you're safer to put up with uneven gloss and color. It will disappear gradually as the paint ages.

Alligatoring

Alligatoring may look okay on alligators, and on shoes and handbags, but on paint . . . never. The defect gets it name because the paint film cracks into segments or islands resembling an alligator's skin. In most cases these cracks don't go through to the wood but involve only the last coat of paint. This shrinks, exposing the coat beneath.

Alligatoring comes from putting a hard-drying coat over an excessively soft one. Don't paint over pitch or tar. Pine and douglas fir commonly used for exterior wood sometimes exudes pitch from pockets, which should be dug out and filled with wood putty before painting. Hard pitch can be removed from the surface by scraping or sanding. Use alcohol to scrub soft pitch, then sand the surface.

Painting over dark-colored trim enamel or red barn paint with white or light-colored house paint may lead to alligatoring. The same is true of painting over shellac or varnish. Always use compatible, or like, paints for good service and follow the manufacturer's directions on the use of primers, etc.

Alligatoring is incurable. If the pattern is fine enough it can be painted over. If the pattern is coarse the only cure is to remove the paint down to bare wood and start over.

Blue Stain

Blue stain is a blue-black discoloration of wood that, under the wrong conditions, can affect any paint put over it. Caused by fungi that grow in damp wood, blue stain is not a form of decay. However, the

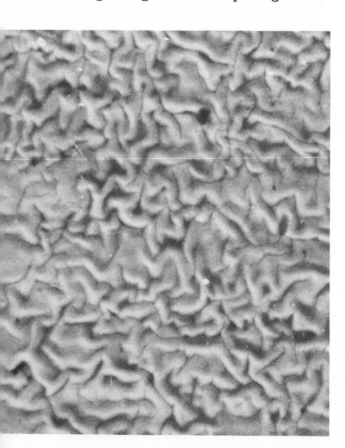

Paint may wrinkle if applied too generously in hot sun. Follow paint's recommended coverage.

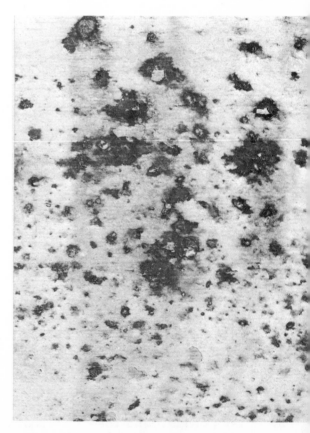

When water-soluble substances in red cedar or redwood leach to surface they discolor. Wash off.

Chalking of paint washes down onto bricks. Poor quality paint used. Needs brushing off, then two coats of quality paint. If latex is used, first coat should be a primer to bond chalky surface.

same wood wetness that favors the growth of blue stain very often leads to the growth of decay-producing fungi.

If wood contains blue stain but in use its moisture content will not be high, the stain can be painted over without danger of further staining. If the wood is likely to be wet for any length of time, blue stain is sure to grow and discolor the new paint.

To prevent blue stain, keep wood dry. Treat unpainted wood with a water repellent preservative. Check gutters and downspouts for leaks. Put a vapor barrier of aluminum oil-base paint on inside walls and ceilings. On wood siding remove paint from the joints that have blue stain and treat them with a water-repellent preservative before repainting.

To remove the discoloration treat blue stain areas with household bleach. Blue stain can also be removed by sanding if the stain doesn't penetrate deeply.

Sulfide Discoloration

Paints containing lead or other metals that form black sulfides are susceptible to sulfide discoloration. It's a defect that's easy to detect. Unlike dirt and mildew, sulfide blackenings usually have a metallic luster that can be bleached with a straight solution of drugstore hydrogen peroxide. Hydrogen sulfide gas, which causes the defect, is most common in industrial areas, particularly around petroleum refineries. It can also come from mineral springs, swamps and polluted streams.

The best preventive for sulfide discoloration is to use paints that don't contain lead. The normal chalking of exterior paint may help.

Crawling

Crawling occurs when there is a drawing back or contraction of freshly spread paint into puddles or drops, the way water acts on a greasy plate. Severe crawling leaves surfaces under the paint exposed. These exposures vary from pinholes to patches.

Crawling is caused by grease, wax, oily dirt or other such substances on the surface. Paint sometimes crawls when a previous paint isn't new enough or weathered enough to receive new paint properly. Sheltered parts of a building may be in this condition when the building is repainted. Paint that is applied to a smooth or glossy surface of an aged paint has a tendency to crawl. Paint applied in cold or humid weather can easily crawl.

Remove greasy substances by sanding or scrubbing with a little ammonia or trisodium phosphate in the wash water to

help. Don't paint over unweathered, young paint. The Forest Products Laboratory recommends repainting weathered surfaces no sooner than at four-year intervals and repainting protected areas every other time (about every eight years). If the old paint is still glossy, wash or sand it before repainting. Don't apply paint in cold or humid weather or to an excessively damp surface. Wait for warm, moderately dry weather and dry surfaces.

Wrinkling

Paint may wrinkle if it is applied too generously, especially in the hot sun. Adding too much oil during mixing will cause wrinkling too, as will a sharp drop in temperature soon after painting.

You can avoid wrinkling by doing your painting in favorable weather and by brushing the paint out well. Follow the manufacturer's recommended coverages.

To save an already-wrinkled paint surface, sand the wrinkles smooth and repaint when the temperature is well above 40° F. Brush the paint out well.

Flaking

This peculiarity of metal painting, in which pieces of paint peel and fall off, is especially common in paint applied over galvanized metal.

To avoid getting a flaky finish on galvanized metal, let the metal weather for at least six months before painting. If this cannot be done, treat the metal as follows: Clean with a grease-removing solvent. Next, pretreat the zinc coating by brushing or swabbing with a solution of ½ pound of copper sulfate (blue vitrol) per gallon of water. Leave the solution on until the metal has changed color, then rinse off with water. Apply a primer that is especially designed for painting galvanized metal. Primers containing zinc dust are usually best. •

Paint Like a

THERE IS A LITTLE MORE to painting than putting on paint. But don't let the ominous sound of that scare you. What we're talking about is the use of aids to painting, things like ladders, tape and various painting tools. Rather than make the job tougher, painting accessories make it easier for you to paint the way professionals do.

Look over the counters of your favorite paint dealer or study the mail order catalogs and you'll find lots of things to help you paint. You could go ape and buy them all, but better to buy just those you really need.

If you don't own the tools and equipment needed to help you work like a pro, they can be rented. Ladders, paint spray outfits, floor sanders, scaffolding are standard items at most tool rental firms. The cost is not great considering the amount of investment it would take to buy everything. For instance, you can rent an aluminum extension ladder for 5 cents a foot minimum or 20 cents a foot for one week. Paint spray outfits rent from $5 to $8 a day depending on their size. A floor sander with edger costs about $9 a day, plus sandpaper. You can rent a 27-foot scaffold for about $10 a day or $30 a week.

Ladders

Painting is a relatively safe pursuit. Aside from the remote possibility of lead and mercury poisoning and the fume and fire dangers, it's pretty hard to get hurt while you're painting—*except on a ladder.* A painting injury is almost always a fall from a ladder. The National Safety Council, that watchful bunch of cats who keep statistics on such things, figure that every year some 12,000 people are killed—not just injured, KILLED—in home falls. More than three times that many are injured. Some of these victims, they reason, were either using ladders incorrectly or were using some substitute for a ladder. Boxes, crates, tubs, chairs, cans make poor stand-ins for a good ladder.

Here is what the safety boys recommend to keep from becoming a fall guy when you use a ladder.

Always inspect a ladder before using it.

You can rent an aluminum extension ladder for 5 cents a foot per day, even cheaper by the week.

National Lead photo

ro

Study your project and decide which are the very best tools and aids needed. Buy some, rent others, and enjoy.

The ladder should be placed on a solid footing, one that isn't slippery. If the ground is soft, put a board under it. Never use a ladder on ice or snow. The bottom of a leaning ladder should be placed one-fourth the ladder length away from the wall. Ladder length is easy to figure because most ladder rungs are one foot apart. Never rest the top of a ladder against a window. Don't set up a ladder in front of a door that is not secured shut, blocked open or guarded by someone.

You may safely reach out to arm's length when painting from a ladder, but no farther. When you must bend your body to reach a spot, you're in the danger zone. Get down and move the ladder.

Never stand on the top two steps of a stepladder or the top three rungs of an extension ladder. Get a longer one, if needed. A ladder should extend 3 feet above the edge of your roof. Overlap between the sections of an extension ladder is important. A ladder up to 36 feet long should have a 3-foot overlap between sections.

Do not extend an extension ladder from the top of the fly section or by bouncing. Don't try to change position by "walking" the ladder while on it. Get down and move it.

Any split, checked, rotted or otherwise deteriorated ladder is like a horse with a broken leg. Much as you dislike to, it must be put out of its misery. Burn it, though, don't shoot it. Never paint a ladder. Paint can cover up signs of deterioration, okay on a house but not on a ladder. You can coat a ladder with linseed oil or varnish if you like.

When a ladder is used on an uneven surface, its low leg should be blocked so that both legs are level.

Always face the ladder when you go up or down. Before going up be sure that your shoes as well as the rungs, are free of dirt, oil, grease or mud. Grip firmly with both hands and put your feet squarely on the rungs. Work facing the ladder and always hold on with one hand. Hook one leg over a rung if you must work with both hands. The paint pail can be hooked over a rung on an S-shaped wire bent from a coat-hanger.

Two on a ladder is ixnay, even if you're married. The extra load may weaken it enough to let it break the next time out.

Before going up a stepladder make sure it's fully opened and that the spreaders are both locked.

A metal ladder should not be used near power lines.

Never use a ladder horizontally as a runway or scaffold. It is not designed for such loads. Store a ladder in a cool dry place away from excessive heat and protected from the elements.

Model 1604

Model 1320-2

A six-ft. ladder is a household necessity. Platform type is most useful. Owner of a two-story home also needs an extension ladder. Buy quality.

Distance ladder must be from house at the bottom for safe use. Add any distance that extends above point of contact or below level of the ground.

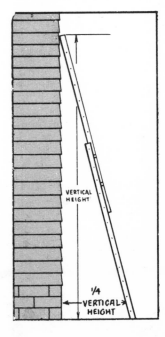

VERTICAL HEIGHT

1/4 VERTICAL HEIGHT

WRONG

Angle too great.
Ladder may break.

WRONG

Base too near house.
Ladder might tip.

WRONG

Top of ladder should
extend two feet
above edge of roof.

RIGHT

Easier and safer to step
from ladder to roof and
back again.

WRONG

Always face a ladder
when ascending or
descending.

RIGHT

Heavy or bulky items
should be lifted by
hoist.

American Ladder Institute

Scuff guards prevent ladder damage to the siding.
Padded sponge protectors slip on and off easily.
Dan-D Products

Types of Ladders

The basic ladder for house painting is the 6-foot stepladder. An 8-footer would be nice for use outdoors, but it is too tall for indoors.

Stepladders are made of wood, aluminum or magnesium. Wooden stepladders should be chosen for durability. Needless to say, the wood used should be free of defects. Metal reinforcing should be sturdy, not looking as though cut from a tin can. The locking bars should be sturdy too and all metal parts should be rust-resistant. The better wood ladders have their dowels mortised into the back rails for added strength. The treads should be cut into the side rails for strength and should be reinforced with metal braces underneath.

The spread at the bottom of a step ladder should be five or six inches for each foot the ladder is tall.

Outdoor painting requires an extension ladder. A one-story house needs a 14-footer. A two-story house often needs a 28-foot ladder. Ladders much longer than that are unmanageable by one person.

Buy top quality. Get a wide ladder for a better footing and more room to work between rails. Rungs must be mortised through the side rails and they should be reinforced with metal. Keep the nuts on reinforcing rods tight. On metal ladders look closely at where the rungs are fastened to the rails. The stronger the better.

Various combination ladders are available. Some convert from stepladders into straight ladders.

For roof and flashing painting a ladder

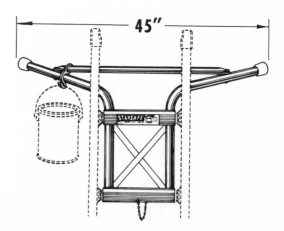

45"

Stand-off brackets increase ladder stability and add to an extension ladder's general usefulness.

hook comes in handy. It fastens to one end of your extension ladder and hooks over the roof gable. For the same purpose you can also get triangular brackets that are nailed under shingles to hold the ladder up.

Scaffolding

If you figure that setting up scaffolding is less trouble than moving a ladder around, go right ahead. It can have advantages when painting where lap marks are troublesome, say in painting a ceiling. With an extension plank between two ladders as a scaffold, you can probably paint all the way across a room without stopping. The extension plank and extra ladder can be purchased or rented.

For outdoor work even more elaborate scaffolds can be useful. Brackets are available to convert a pair of extension ladders into something you can lay a plank between. You can then work from the plank. Also available are metal brackets that nail to the house studs from outside the wall. Planks can be laid across the brackets. The trouble with this method is the nasty holes that have to be filled when you remove the scaffolding.

If you like carpentry, you can bang up an admirable scaffold out of 2 x 4's or 4 x 4's, using 1 x 6 cross braces on all four sides. An 8-foot-long, 4-foot-wide wooden scaffold can be moved around the house as you work. Height can be up to 8 feet. It's best to have a safety rail extending up another 4 feet or so to keep you from taking that first step that's a lulu.

Really tall scaffolds can be built but you'd better consult a good book on carpentry to see how they are nailed and braced.

If you're rental-minded, you can rent a set of pump-jacks that work on a pair of 2 x 4's braced out from the house walls. Planks laid between the pair of jacks can be raised merely by jacking with your foot.

You can also rent a steel or aluminum scaffold in heights from 6 to 27 feet and more.

Check out any scaffold before you use it to be sure it's sturdy, free of knotty or defective planks, level and solidly placed. Follow the instructions to the letter when assembling metal scaffolding. Check the guard rails for safety. The top rail should be 3 to 4 feet above the deck.

Never let the unsupported end of a plank extend very far to where one unguarded step and you'll have visions without LSD.

Don't use ladders or other devices on top of scaffolds to increase their height.

Provide adequate support for the legs of a scaffold or you may find yourself clinging to a leaning tower of Pisa.

Masking

Part of painting like a pro is knowing how to use masking tape. Masking tape, or more precisely *pressure-sensitive* masking tape, is made of crinkly crepe paper that has been filled with rubber to give it a controlled amount of stretch and strength. Its adhesives are mostly rubber that has been made permanently tacky. Masking tape sticks on contact with just a little pressure, hence the *pressure-sensitive* tag or label.

Make moist but not wet tack rag by adding turps and varnish to old wash cloth. Keep it in a jar.

Plastic bleach bottle makes good brush or paint holder. Cut with knife, tip of soldering gun.

Masking tape comes off as easily as it goes on. A light pull strips it off clean. The general idea in using masking tape is to cover areas that you don't want painted. If they're wider than the tape, you can use tape in conjunction with paper. A piece of newspaper will do. Masking tape comes in many widths. I've found the ¾-inch width the most useful around home.

Masking tape will stick to any surface that is clean, dry, free of grease, etc.

An easy way to apply paper with tape is to pretape the paper. Lay down the paper and stretch masking tape along one edge, half on the paper and half off. Then pick up the taped paper and stick it wherever you want it.

When using masking tape to get a straight, clean line between two colors of paint, paint the first color slightly beyond the two-tone line. Let it dry thoroughly so that taping will not damage it, then apply taped paper along the line, covering up the first color. You can paint the second color right over the tape. But be sure the tape edges are stuck down tight. You can see to this by sliding the bowl of a spoon or your thumbnail along the edge.

The sooner you remove masking tape the better. Usually tape should be peeled off when the paint has set or becomes tacky. If the paint shows no tendency to run, and you avoid smears, you can remove it as soon as you're through painting.

In any case, don't let the tape stay in place as long as two or three days. As the paint film becomes tougher, there is a greater chance of tearing a jagged edge as you pull off tape. Maximum removal time varies with the type of paint you use—latexes dry very quickly.

To make stripes the same width as the tape, apply tape and merely paint over it. Double-check both edges to be sure the tape is stuck down tightly. Otherwise paint may creep under it. Strip it off when you're finished painting.

For a wide stripe use two strips of tape with paper between.

Masking window glass is not difficult with masking tape. You can either cut the tape at corners or go around them neatly

Displays of painting accessories in your dealer's store will suggest tools needed for your next job.

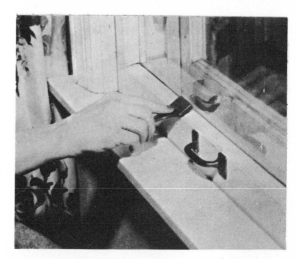

Sash tool is a sponge with handle. It allows the paint to cover sash without getting any on glass.

The screen-painting tool shown here is simply a carpet-like pad to be dipped in paint and applied.

by making a fold of the excess tape. Don't leave masking tape on the window for too many days. It tends to bake onto the glass. Then removal is tough.

Masking of curves should not be done with tape that is too wide to make the bends. The tighter the bend the narrower the tape should be. Narrow widths, such as ½-inch, will negotiate the curves easily, then you can follow with wider tape and paper, if needed for full masking.

Little But Useful Tools

A number of accessories are made to help you greatly in around-the-house painting.

Extra large paint pail—Holds more than a gallon, enabling you to pour a gallon of paint in and have room for stirring, brush-dipping, etc.

Disposable paint tray insert—Drop one of these into your regular roller tray and the messy tray clean-up is ended. Ash-can it when you finish. Available in 7-inch and 9-inch tray sizes.

Paint roller pail—Great for working from a ladder with a paint roller, this gadget takes the place of the standard roller tray. It holds up to 2 gallons of paint and hangs neatly from a wire.

Pail hook—A sturdy metal hook to hang a paint pail on ladder rungs, etc.

Dropcloth—Made in both plastic and cloth, a dropcloth is a basic cover-up accessory for indoor or outdoor painting. Every home painter needs at least one. The cloth kind are tougher, more resistant to tearing. The plastic ones, available in 1-mil and stronger 2-mil thicknesses, are much cheaper.

Razor blade scraper—A single-edge razor blade mounted in a convenient handle is used for removing paint from around window panes and such. The blade usually folds in for safe keeping.

Roller-scraper—For windows, it strips paint off the glass without digging into the putty. Rollers see to that.

Paint scraper—There are two types: hooked-blade and straight-blade. The hooked-blade type is for heavy paint-removing jobs while the straight-blade type is for lightly scraping.

Dan-D Products

Polyethylene paint roller pail takes place of the roller tray, holds more, handles easier on ladder.

A disc sander is a real pro tool when faced with sanding down to bare wood or bare metal in spots.

For large surfaces, a belt sander with various grits is one of most useful tools you can have.
Black & Decker

New hand-held tape dispenser lets you "drive" the tape onto surface where you want it for masking.
Unipat Co.

Disposable gloves—A boon to the evening or weekend painter in keeping paint-splotched hands from squealing to friends at the office about your extracurricular activities.

Paint shield—A thin metal strip with a handle, it keeps you from painting floors, trim, windows, etc., while you are painting wall surfaces next to them.

Sanding pad—Various sizes hold sandpaper for easier hand-sanding. One kind stores the paper in a roll at one end.

Extension roller handle—Fastens to a paint roller handle letting you paint floors without stooping, ceilings without a ladder.

Ladder scuff guard—Soft tips that slip over the ends of a straight ladder keep it from damaging the house walls when leaned against them.

Disposable paint applicators—Polyurethane sponges mounted on wood handles, these brush substitutes are available in various widths for use with all paints except shellac and lacquers. They can be trimmed with scissors to fit any spot.

Corner applicator—A sponge pad mounted on rollers, this tool is designed to help you paint an inside corner such as between the wall and ceiling without getting any paint on the other surface. It leaves a neat, straight line.

Shingle-shake-siding painter—This applicator is a flat sponge-like pad that is dipped into paint and used to spread it.

Sash applicator—A small sponge applicator designed for painting window sash.

Paint striping kit—Used for putting stripes of various widths on furniture, autos, etc., the paint flows from a small bottle onto a roller. A wire guide bar lets you follow a straightedge or curve.

Brush-cleaning comb—Similar to a hair comb but made of metal, a brush-cleaning comb is useful for removing softened paint that is lodged in a brush's bristles.

Roller-cleaning tool—The curved part of this tool is shaped to fit the curve of the roller and is used to work excess paint out of the roller nap without getting solvent on your fingers.

Estimator rule—A spring steel rule that instantly snaps into a 6-foot rigid length and can be made to snap back automatically into a 1¾-inch coil. One side of the rule is printed with estimating suggestions and charts.

Window opener—Serrated blade can be worked between the paint-covered crevices around a window with a sawing action to loosen a stuck sash.

Painting tape—A one-piece masking paper with adhesive edge in a dispenser pack. The manufacturer claims that it cuts masking time in half over the use of tape and paper.

Tack rag—Indispensable in picking up dust and lint just before putting on a fine finish, a tack rag is sticky but does not leave a residue on the surface.

Taped-paper masking is an easy way to paint that straight line in two-tone. Peel off immediately.

Mask a window pane by folding a sheet of newspaper slightly smaller than glass and taping it.

Paint spatula—Made with spring steel blades for adding and stirring tinting colors, spatulas are available in blade widths from 3x½-inch to 14x1¾-inch.

This is by no means a complete list of all the painting accessories available. Nor does it mean that you will need every item listed. Choose only the ones necessary to help you paint like a pro.

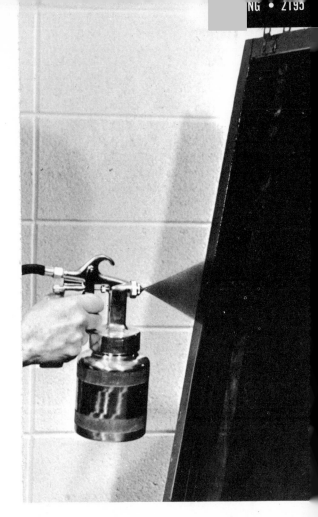

One way to make renting a spray outfit pay off is to save your small spray paint chores.

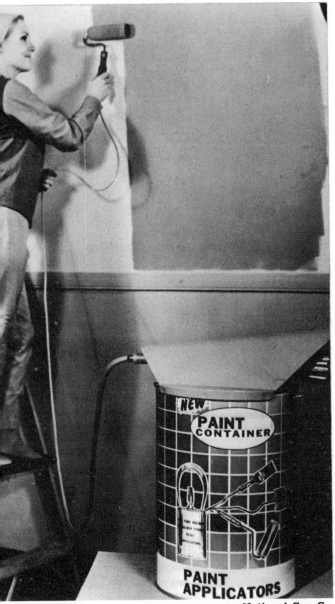

National Can Co.

Trayless roller painting is now possible with a new pressure-fed system. Can be carried on shoulder.

For big jobs like long fences, barns, even house exteriors, consider renting a spray gun with tank.

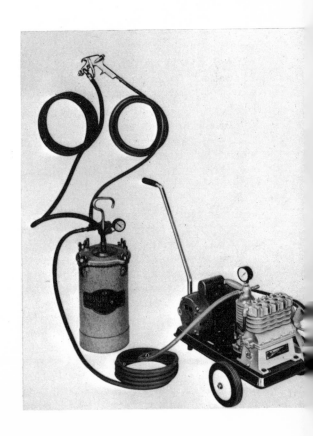

A 100 percent solids coating would go on thickly, smooth to a glassy surface and would not shrink.

Newest Developments

THE IDEAL PAINT would come in an aerosol can. It would paint a whole house merely by spraying it at the house from ten feet away. The spray would be self-masking, not even sticking to areas that you didn't want painted. The coating would be impervious as stainless steel to sunlight, water, acids, dirt, mildew and wear. One coat would last a lifetime. Colors, 1000 of them in gloss, semi-gloss and flat, would be available at every paint dealer for $1.98 per can. A deluxe aerosol at $2.25 would push the button for you.

You shouldn't laugh. Stranger predictions have come true. Even in the more immediate future we can look for some startling developments in paints. Two recent ones of the past have been the semi-gloss latex and the development by Du Pont of a no-primer latex house paint.

Long the goal of the paint industry has been a *100 percent solids coating*. Such a paint would contain pigment and vehicle as usual. But there would be no thinner to evaporate. A 100 percent solids coating would go on thickly, flow to a glass-smooth surface and not shrink upon drying. One coat would cover what now takes two. Most catalytic coatings—among them epoxy and polyurethane—approach being 100 percent solids paints, but contain some volatile solvents. The true 100 percent solids coating is still a dream, as far as the consumer is concerned.

Manufacturers are working on new types of exterior paints, ones more like the baked-on paints used on prefabricated metal siding. One approach is through new methods of curing house paint by heat and catalysts, the way epoxies are cured. Then the hardness and durability of a factory-baked finish could be produced in an air-drying house paint.

Some day an exterior clear finish that will outlast present-day house paints is sure to be produced. Steady improvements in polyurethanes may bring it about. Or it may take some other route.

Curing a paint job with heat and catalysts for a "factory" finish will eliminate this process.

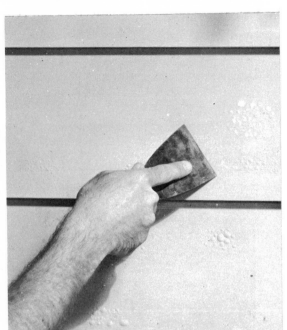

Two recent blessings have been the development of semigloss latex and a no-primer house paint.

n Paints

Manufacturers are working toward the goal of an ideal and inexpensive paint.

Look for much more use of plastics in improved paints. Rohm and Haas is soon expected to release an acrylic resin for latex paints that would be self-priming over metal. Others under development.

A big movement in the paint industry is toward factory-applied coatings. The big advantage is quality control. Flooring, siding, wall paneling, ceiling tile and hardboard are already produced with factory paints.

Home appliances are going to be finished more like fine furniture. The day may come soon when you can order your new washer in bleached walnut. Home appliances are going to get further away from the all-alike painted look.

National Lead is working on a new rust-preventive paint system in which the primer would double as the finish coat, with no loss in protection. Du Pont is developing a unique primer based on barium lanolate. Very low in water-soluble salts, it is not penetrated greatly by water.

Soon to be released is an acrylic resin for latex paints that will even be self-priming over metal.

SIDEWINDER

By Hal Kelly

This paddle wheel boat is a barrel of fun for the kids—build it for less than $35.

BUILDING this boat will really put you in solid with the small fry—*if* you will give them a chance to play with it when it's finished. And the job takes no more than a weekend for anyone who can cut wood along a line. You don't even need power tools, though they're great for doing a fast job. Study plans carefully, then go to work.

When it comes to moving the boat, Junior needs only a few minutes of practice before he's in complete control. A four-year-old can do it and my own six-year-old can make her go faster than an adult can row a boat. There's no front or back—she goes just as well in either direction—and she'll spin around on a floating leaf if the cranks

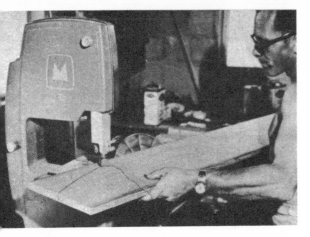

SIDES and centerpiece have same curves but are cut separately; it's too awkward to join the three and cut them together.

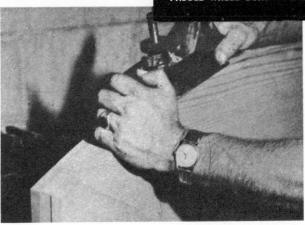

WHEN CUT, the three are joined temporarily and planed to equal shape; check with square to be sure sides are 90° to edges.

are turned in opposite directions. It's great fun and a safe boat, too.

No jig is necessary for construction. The sides and center section are cut to the dimensions shown and, since they have the same bottom curve, are clamped together for planing. They must match exactly on the underside, with the edges square to the sides, so that the bottom will lie flush on all three. When this is done, the end pieces are cut to size and then dadoed at the center and rabbeted at the ends to half their depth. Then the whole frame can be assembled with waterproof glue and 1¼-inch No. 8 screws. Addition of an exterior plywood bottom completes the hull except for the center gussets, the seat framing and the seats. Before adding the seats, apply one coat of white Firzite and two coats of exterior enamel.

The paddles are easily constructed of ¼-inch exterior plywood and solid stock. They're assembled with glue and ¾-inch No. 16 Anchorfast nails and painted in the same manner as the hull. Ours are bright red to match the seats and contrast nicely with a white hull.

SABER SAW is used for making cutouts in center section; this tool can be used for all the cuts if band saw isn't available.

FRAME is assembled with glue and screws; the end pieces are dadoed and rabbeted to take center section and sides respectively.

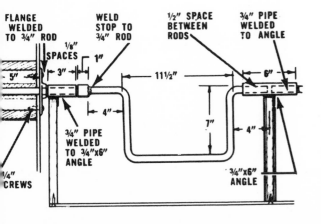

FLANGE WELDED TO ¾" ROD

WELD STOP TO ¾" ROD

½" SPACE BETWEEN RODS

¾" PIPE WELDED TO ANGLE

⅛" SPACES

1"

3"

5"

11½"

6"

4"

¾" PIPE WELDED TO ¾"x6" ANGLE

7"

4"

¾"x6" ANGLE

¼" CREWS

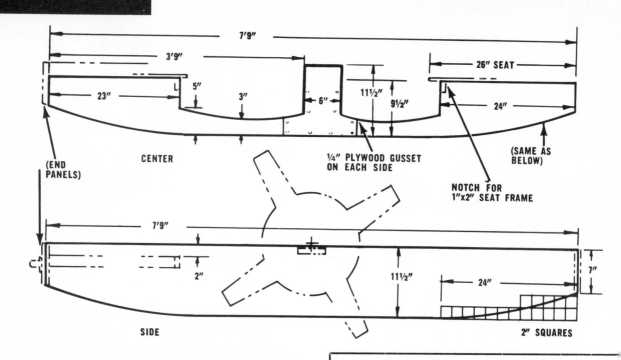

7'9"
3'9"
26" SEAT
5"
23"
3"
6"
11½"
9½"
24"
CENTER
¼" PLYWOOD GUSSET ON EACH SIDE
(SAME AS BELOW)
(END PANELS)
NOTCH FOR 1"x2" SEAT FRAME

7'9"
2"
11½"
24"
7"
SIDE
2" SQUARES

LARGE SCALE PLANS

will greatly simplify construction of this boat, SIDEWINDER. Please consult your PLANS REFERENCE LISTING for the exact source and price. Refer to Plan Number 141.

BOTTOM is ¼-in. plywood which is glued and screwed down, starting at the center and working alternately toward each end.

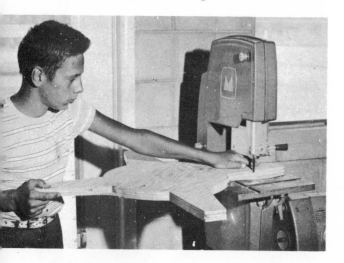

PADDLE WHEEL sides can be cut with a band saw in one operation if four pieces of ½-in. exterior plywood are sandwiched.

PAINT JOB is begun before seats are in place. All woodwork gets a coat of white Firzite and two coats of exterior enamel.

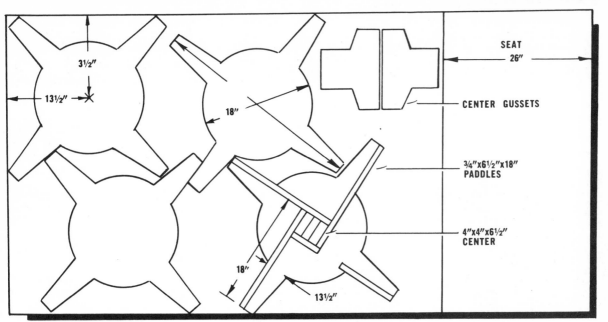

PARTS FROM ONE ¼"x4'x8' EXTERIOR PLYWOOD SHEET

The best approach to building the cranks is to have the local metal shop make them up. They'll have the angle iron and ¾-inch metal rod in stock. When the flanges and the stops are welded to the rods, be sure that a ⅛-inch space is allowed between them and the pipe bearings. My total cost for the crank material and labor was under eight dollars.

Study the drawings and photographs and get to work. You'll look far and wide before you find another project which provides so much fun for kids at so little labor and cost. •

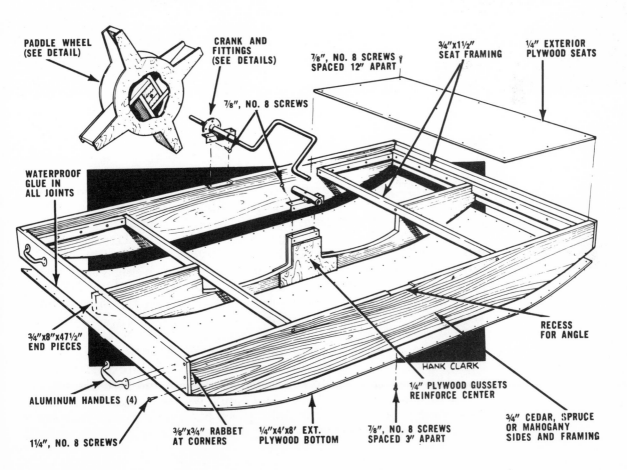

HOW TO INSTALL
KNOTTY PINE WALLS

By J. Robert Connor

THE SOFT, rustic warmth of wood-paneled walls will enhance the interior of any home. The installation of wood panels for the walls of a living room, rumpus room, basement or den does require some effort on the part of the homeowner. However, the final results are well worth the labor involved.

The paneling we chose for our dining room-living room area was solid ¾-inch-thick tongue-and-groove Idaho White Pine, a straight-grained, soft and even wood that is light in color. Idaho White Pine is one of the ten species available from the Western Pine Association, 526 American Bank Building, Portland, Ore. 97205. The other species available from Western Pine are Ponderosa Pine, Sugar Pine, Douglas Fir, Larch, White Fir, Engelmann Spruce, Lodgepole Pine, Incense Cedar and Red Cedar.

All species come in 6, 8, 10 and 12-inch widths and are available in a variety of patterns. Paneling can be installed in a number of ways—vertically, horizontally, diagonally, etc.

STRAIGHT-EDGE member should be placed against horizontal furring strips to make sure they are flush. If not, shim so that panels will be uniform.

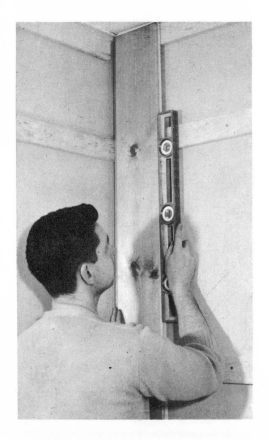

TRIM the grooved edge of the first board and secure it in the corner of the room. It should be plumb. Use your level to be certain that it is.

Once it was decided that Idaho White Pine was going to be our choice, we visited the local lumber yard to examine and order the boards. We selected the eight-inch wide, eight-foot long panels in uniform widths. Panels also can be ordered in random widths to create an unusual effect.

When the paneling is delivered, it should be stored for several days in the room where it is to be used. Separating sticks should be used between each piece so that the wood can adjust to the room's normal humidity conditions. This is to prevent warping.

The first step is to sand and stain each panel *before* it goes on the wall. Staining before installation makes it possible for you to cover hard-to-reach places that you might not be able to reach when the boards are in place. We used Minwax Wood Finish No. 230, Early American. Stain was applied to each panel with a brush, then wiped off. The result was a light stain with a soft finish.

When the panels are dry you're ready to begin the major part of the job. Remove all molding around windows and doors. Since our paneling was going to be installed vertically, we nailed four 1x4-inch furring strips horizontally across each wall. However, a wider nailing strip can be used at the base so that the paneling and baseboard have a flush surface. Furring strips also have to be nailed around all doors and windows. Allow enough room for inch or half-inch pieces of wood to be nailed around the inside frames of the doors and windows so that the trim molding can be nailed on later.

If you panel over framing, no nailing strips will be necessary—if you run the boards horizontally. If you panel over framing on exterior walls in a new house, insulation should be used.

When the four horizontal furring strips have been nailed on the walls, take a straight piece of lumber and hold it vertically against the furring strips. The furring strips should all touch the vertically-held member. Shim any places that are not flush. This is important as the paneling should be flush with the furring strips to eliminate bulges along the wall.

Each piece of board should be pre-cut to fit. Trim the grooved edge of the first board and start in a corner of the room. Make certain that this first panel is plumb by checking it with your level. Now blind-

WAYS TO TRIM WINDOWS AND DOORS—SHOWN IN CROSS SECTION

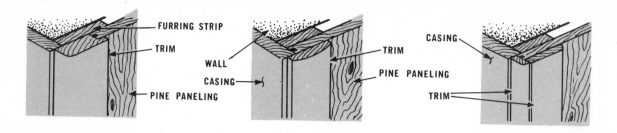

FURRING STRIP
TRIM
PINE PANELING

WALL
CASING
TRIM
PINE PANELING

CASING
TRIM

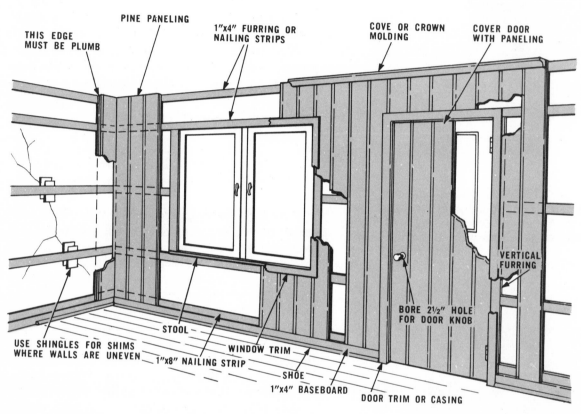

THIS EDGE MUST BE PLUMB
PINE PANELING
1"x4" FURRING OR NAILING STRIPS
COVE OR CROWN MOLDING
COVER DOOR WITH PANELING
VERTICAL FURRING
BORE 2½" HOLE FOR DOOR KNOB
USE SHINGLES FOR SHIMS WHERE WALLS ARE UNEVEN
STOOL
WINDOW TRIM
1"x8" NAILING STRIP
SHOE
1"x4" BASEBOARD
DOOR TRIM OR CASING

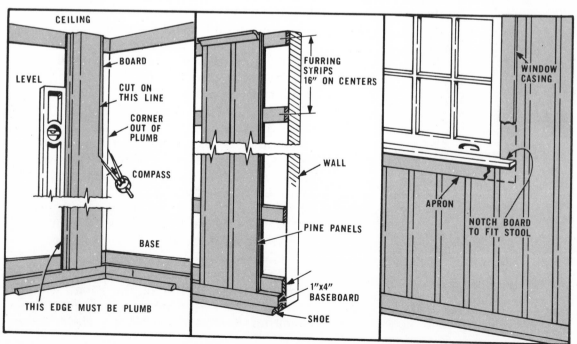

CEILING
BOARD
CUT ON THIS LINE
CORNER OUT OF PLUMB
LEVEL
COMPASS
BASE
THIS EDGE MUST BE PLUMB

FURRING STRIPS 16" ON CENTERS
WALL
PINE PANELS
1"x4" BASEBOARD
SHOE

WINDOW CASING
APRON
NOTCH BOARD TO FIT STOOL

HOW TO INSTALL KNOTTY PINE WALLS

BLIND-NAIL finishing brads through the tongue of each panel and into the furring strips. Then countersink the brads.

SCRAP piece of board can be used to lock tongue and groove. Use hammer lightly so as not to damage wood.

PANELS were nailed directly to the doors. Power saw was used to cut excess wood.

nail with brads through the tongue and into the furring strips. Countersink all nails. It is also a good idea to put nails into the top and bottom of each board. They will be covered by the trim molding.

The groove of the next board is now inserted into the tongue of the panel already in place. The groove of the new board should fit snugly into the tongue of the first one, concealing the nail holes. If you run into a stubborn piece, take some scrap board and insert the groove into the tongue of the panel. Lightly tap the scrap piece with your hammer. This will close the tongue and groove of the adjacent panels.

When you start on the second wall of the room, trim the groove again and butt the new panel against the one already installed. For outside corners you'll have to miter the ends. If surface-nailing is necessary countersink the nails and fill the holes with putty mixed with the same stain used on the wood. Boards should be cut to fit around doors and windows. Don't forget to make cut-outs for all electrical outlets.

Furring strips also can be nailed to the doors in the room and the panels secured. However, we found it easier to fasten the boards directly to the doors. When the paneling was completed the doors were simply moved forward on their hinges and re-hung so they were flush with the walls.

When the panels are up, the protective finish should be applied. We put on two coats of shellac—two parts of shellac to one part of denatured alcohol. After each coat was brushed on and had dried, the walls were rubbed lightly with No. 2 steel wool. Then a final coat of Valspar Soft Gloss No. 11 varnish was put on with a brush.

When this job was finished we returned to the doors. The old locks had been removed when the doors were paneled. New holes had to be drilled to take the heavy-duty series C locks made by the Schlage Lock Company of San Francisco, Calif. The locks were changed because the old ones were not long enough to fit through the almost-three-inch doors. They come with a template and installation instructions and a special tool to secure them.

Paneling added to existing walls, as in this project, adds to the insulation of an older house. There is a one-inch air space between the wall and the ¾-inch thick panels.

When the project is complete the walls will require only an occasional dusting with cloth or vacuum cleaner. When it becomes necessary, they can be cleaned with a soft damp cloth and a solution of mild soap and warm water

This is a one-time installation which will not only enhance the beauty of your home but also increase its value. •

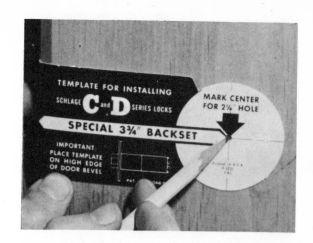

SCHLAGE heavy-duty series C locks were installed in living room-dining room doors.

HALF-INCH drill was used to make new holes in door. This should be done with care.

BEFORE SHOT shows walls without paneling. Note difference in lead photo of story.

CRAYON marks can be wiped off the Marlite door panel with a damp cloth.

PLAYTIME DOOR PANEL

When is a door not a door?
—when it's a display board in
your little girl's own room!

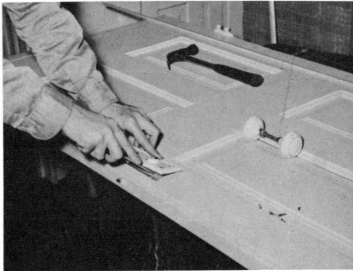

A FINISHING touch would be to replace the old door knob with a newer one of modern design.

LET your little girl or boy write all over the door of his or her room. A piece of plastic-surfaced Marlite will provide a surface that, unlike the walls, is washable. Children can draw or write on the hard surface and wipe it right off with a cloth. A piece of cork or insulating board mounted on the door above the Marlite will make a good pin-up bulletin board and make the door do double duty.

The project can be completed quickly and easily because no work has to be done on the door. Take the door off the hinges (by removing the hinge pins) and remove the knob and any hardware. If the door is a panel-type, fill in any depressions with cardboard so that the Marlite lies flat across.

Do not remove door hinges. The molding should be flush with the hinges as well as flush with the other three sides.

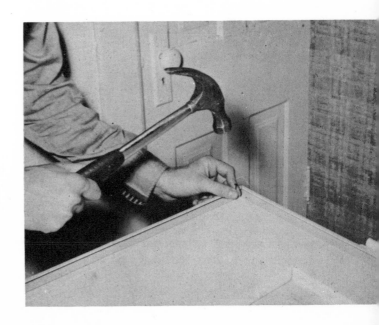

GLUE and nail the molding strips flush to the edge all around the door.

patio dining set

It has a removable chair for children, a charcoal brazier in the center

IF YOUR guests have trouble climbing over the seat of your old-fashioned patio picnic table, here's a graceful solution. Build this curved table and bench set.

The table and benches have a premium quality look but their cost is moderate when high density overlaid fir plywood is used.

The bench frames and table legs are cut from two thicknesses of ¾-inch thick high density overlaid fir plywood and laminated together. High density plywood is also used for the bench backs, seats, and table top.

The benches and table are eight feet long.

Six people can be seated on each bench with room to spare. A "plus" feature is a hole in the center of the table which holds a habachi charcoal brazier. With the habachi, foods can be kept hot or steaks grilled right at the table.

The benches conform to the curved edges of the table for a well-designed look. You can also make a detachable chair for a youngster which can be clamped to the end of the table. It is an ingenious combination of a metal framework with a plywood seat and back. •

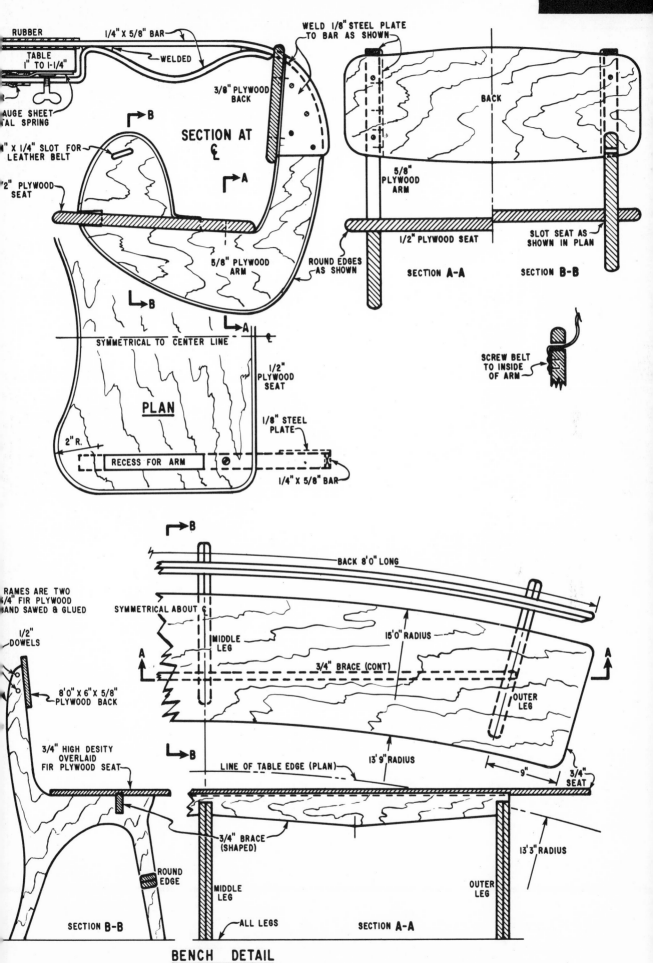

RUBBER

1/4" X 5/8" BAR

WELD 1/8" STEEL PLATE
TO BAR AS SHOWN

WELDED

TABLE
1" TO 1-1/4"

AUGE SHEET
TAL SPRING

" X 1/4" SLOT FOR
LEATHER BELT

3/8" PLYWOOD
BACK

SECTION AT ₵

2" PLYWOOD
SEAT

5/8" PLYWOOD
ARM

ROUND EDGES
AS SHOWN

SYMMETRICAL TO CENTER LINE

1/2"
PLYWOOD
SEAT

PLAN

2" R.

RECESS FOR ARM

1/8" STEEL
PLATE

1/4" X 5/8" BAR

BACK

5/8"
PLYWOOD
ARM

1/2" PLYWOOD SEAT

SECTION A-A

SLOT SEAT AS
SHOWN IN PLAN

SECTION B-B

SCREW BELT
TO INSIDE
OF ARM

BACK 8'0" LONG

RAMES ARE TWO
/4" FIR PLYWOOD
AND SAWED & GLUED

SYMMETRICAL ABOUT ₵

MIDDLE
LEG

15'0" RADIUS

1/2"
DOWELS

3/4" BRACE (CONT)

OUTER
LEG

8'0" X 6"X 5/8"
PLYWOOD BACK

3/4" HIGH DESITY
OVERLAID
FIR PLYWOOD SEAT

13'9" RADIUS

LINE OF TABLE EDGE (PLAN)

9"

3/4"
SEAT

3/4" BRACE
(SHAPED)

ROUND
EDGE

13'3" RADIUS

MIDDLE
LEG

OUTER
LEG

SECTION B-B

ALL LEGS

SECTION A-A

BENCH DETAIL

DIAGRAM SHOWN HERE gives dimensions for table top. Highlight of this patio set is the habachi or charcoal brazier built into the center of the table for warming or even cooking simple dishes while the meal is in progress. (You can build the table without the brazier, however.) Table is made from high density resin overlaid fir plywood in a gray green color tone unpainted or finished in any way. The overlay is a hard, clear, glass-smooth, extremely abrasion resistant surface which is ideal for this application.

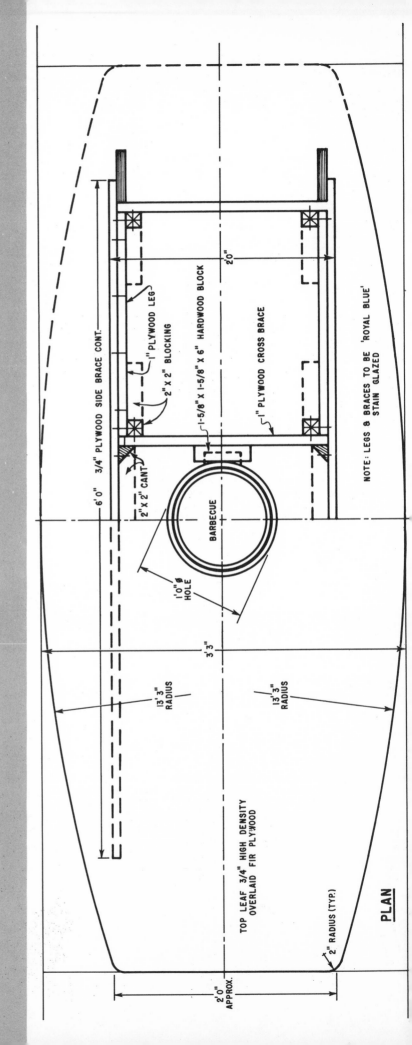

3/4" PLYWOOD SIDE BRACE CONT.

1" PLYWOOD LEG

2" x 2" BLOCKING

1-5/8" x 1-5/8" x 6" HARDWOOD BLOCK

1" PLYWOOD CROSS BRACE

2'0"

6'0"

2" x 2" CANT

BARBECUE

1'0" Ø HOLE

NOTE: LEGS & BRACES TO BE 'ROYAL BLUE' STAIN GLAZED

3'3"

13'3" RADIUS

13'3" RADIUS

TOP LEAF 3/4" HIGH DENSITY OVERLAID FIR PLYWOOD

2" RADIUS (TYP.)

2'0" APPROX.

PLAN

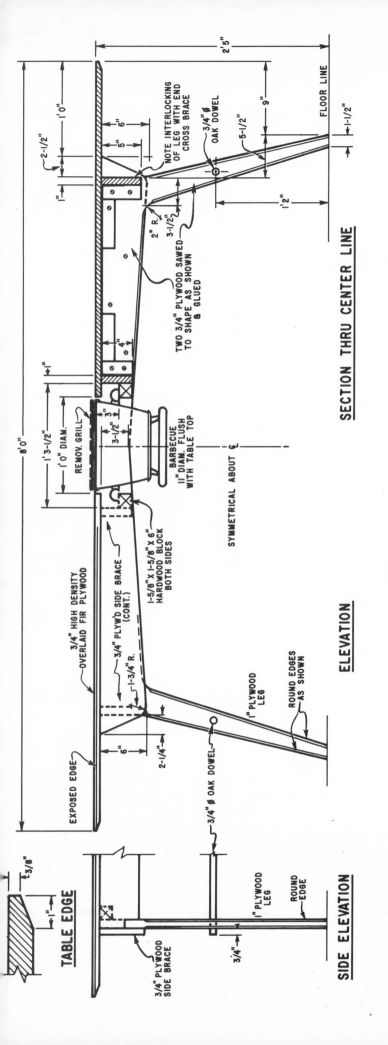

TABLE EDGE

3/8"

1"

SIDE ELEVATION

3/4" PLYWOOD SIDE BRACE

3/4"

1" PLYWOOD LEG

ROUND EDGE

ELEVATION

8'0"

EXPOSED EDGE

3/4" HIGH DENSITY OVERLAID FIR PLYWOOD

3/4" PLYW'D SIDE BRACE (CONT.)

1-3/4" R.

6"

2-1/4"

3/4" ⌀ OAK DOWEL

1" PLYWOOD LEG

ROUND EDGES AS SHOWN

1-5/8" X 1-5/8" X 6" HARDWOOD BLOCK BOTH SIDES

SYMMETRICAL ABOUT ₵

REMOV. GRILL

1'0" DIAM.

1'3-1/2"

1"

3-1/2"

3"

BARBECUE 11" DIAM. FLUSH WITH TABLE TOP

SECTION THRU CENTER LINE

2'5"

1'0"

2-1/2"

1"

6"

5"

NOTE INTERLOCKING OF LEG WITH END CROSS BRACE

3/4" ⌀ OAK DOWEL

9"

5-1/2"

FLOOR LINE

1-1/2"

1'2"

2" R.

3-1/2"

TWO 3/4" PLYWOOD SAWED TO SHAPE AS SHOWN & GLUED

4"

DIAGRAM SHOWN HERE gives elevation dimensions for the table. It also gives details for installation of charcoal burner, if you desire to put unit into table. Both table and benches will have a premium quality look when completed, but their cost is moderate when high density overlaid fir plywood is used. High density plywood has a hard smooth translucent surface which is achieved at the plywood mill by fusing a sheet of resin fiber to a plywood panel under great heart and extreme pressure.

Weatherproof Your Patio

By David A. Howard

Corrugated glass-fiber patio roof sheds rain,
provides warm, diffused light even on dull days.

EXCEPT for the severe winter months, suburban living is simply other words for outdoor living. Like most suburbanites, my wife, my children and I relax, eat our meals and entertain our guests in the favorite part of our home—the patio.

But, because we had an open patio, the weather was a problem. Rain kept the family reluctantly indoors; too bright sunlight made relaxing uncomfortable.

The answer was a roof—but what kind of a roof? A standard, shingle covered roof would cut out too much light and make both our kitchen and dining room area too dark. What was needed was a roof made of a strong, translucent, building material that could withstand all kinds of weather conditions. After inquiry and study of various types of structural material we decided on Corrulux, panels of

Raised patio was built within block walls. Red slates and small colored ceramic tiles were leveled on reinforced concrete floor.

A patio roof of corrugated panels of brightly colored glass fiber makes for comfortable outdoor living, and adds beauty to your home.

corrugated lightweight sheets made of resins and Fiberglas. Of the colors available, we selected Sunlight Yellow to compliment the color scheme of our house and surroundings.

The patio itself, which we had finished earlier, was constructed by building walls of cement blocks set on a footing three feet below the ground. Fill was thrown into the cavity formed by the walls and covered with a layer of sand. The patio cement floor was then poured, using heavy wire mesh for strength. Red slate and "sprinkles" of small ceramic tiles were set in cement surface to enliven the effect. The concrete block walls were capped with green pre-colored commercial cement bricks, and small holes were left at the joint between every second brick for drainage.

We ordered enough 40-inch-wide panels of Corrulux to cover our 14x26-foot patio —half in 8-foot lengths and half in 6-foot lengths. We decided on 4x4-inch posts, 2x6-inch rafters. Cross rafters would have to be cut in short sections, called cats, and toe-nailed in place rather than have one long rafter set in notches, since any cuts into the slanting rafters would tend to weaken them. Thinner, 1x2-inch short pieces were finally installed at both the top leading edge and just behind the bottom leading edge to prevent twisting or warping. Heavier cats at these points would look out of proportion.

We decided a good way to fasten the three 7-foot posts to the surface of the patio would be to use ¼x2x8-inch strips of brass. These were sunk into 5-inch holes (routed out with a carbide-tipped masonry drill)

Since 40-inch-wide fiber panels were to overlap one corrugation, this provided 37⅜-inch centers which dictated position of rafters. Centers were marked on 2x6 plate to be mounted on house wall and notches were cut in plate to accept rafters.

Wall or back plate was positioned under eaves so that notches fit under centers already marked on molding. Allowance had to be made under eaves for height of rafters plus roof panels, then plate was temporarily nailed to the wall.

The 26-foot back plate was put up in two 13-foot sections. Two holes were sunk through plate into every hidden 16-inch centers of wall studding for 5-inch lag screws. After screws were tightened back plate was painted same color as house wall.

A carbide-tipped masonry drill was used to make holes in the patio concrete floor in which metal anchors were to be imbedded to hold the 4x4-inch roof supporting posts. To avoid the problems of rust, it was decided to use brass bars for anchors.

Brass anchors for each of three supporting posts were set in 5-inch holes, and held in place with lead solder. Blowtorch readily melted bar of lead to fill hole. To make sure of firmness, the hole was drilled larger at the bottom than at top.

Slots were drilled in the bottom of 4x4-inch posts and the ends were treated with a wood preservative and painted. At upper left, the posts were then set in place over projecting brass anchor bar and held in position temporarily.

First of three 7-foot roof supporting posts, all of which had been notched at the top to receive the outer header plate, is placed in line with square, and vertical level, and held in true position by stakes clamped tightly to the beam.

Since three supporting posts were to be used to hold the forward weight of the patio roof the procedure was first to align two outside posts, then to clamp temporary crossbeams along frontage to put middle post in position.

The 2x6-inch front header plate was clamped across three posts to check alignment. Front top edge of posts were previously notched to accept this 2x6-inch plate. Rafters may now be placed across top and measured for cutting.

After correct spacing for rafter centers had been marked on header plate, it was dismounted. Below, the first rafter was set in notch in back plate, and it was measured for placement on end post, using a dummy header plate.

Photo at bottom right shows position of two header plates and post. Front header rests on notch in post. Inside header is clamped so that bottom of rafters butt against both plates. Two stove bolts hold them together.

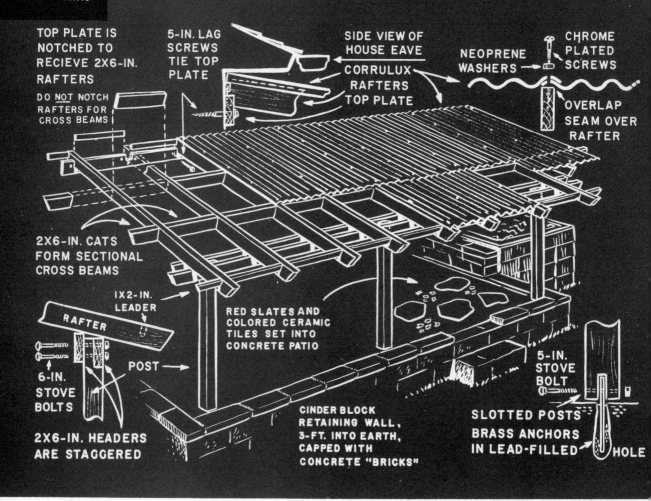

TOP PLATE IS NOTCHED TO RECIEVE 2X6-IN. RAFTERS

DO NOT NOTCH RAFTERS FOR CROSS BEAMS

5-IN. LAG SCREWS TIE TOP PLATE

SIDE VIEW OF HOUSE EAVE

CORRULUX RAFTERS TOP PLATE

NEOPRENE WASHERS

CHROME PLATED SCREWS

OVERLAP SEAM OVER RAFTER

2X6-IN. CATS FORM SECTIONAL CROSS BEAMS

1X2-IN. LEADER

RAFTER

RED SLATES AND COLORED CERAMIC TILES SET INTO CONCRETE PATIO

POST

6-IN. STOVE BOLTS

5-IN. STOVE BOLT

2X6-IN. HEADERS ARE STAGGERED

CINDER BLOCK RETAINING WALL, 3-FT. INTO EARTH, CAPPED WITH CONCRETE "BRICKS"

SLOTTED POSTS BRASS ANCHORS IN LEAD-FILLED HOLE

and held in place with melted lead. A small blowtorch was used here. Slots to receive the projecting 3-inch sections of brass were cut into the bottoms of the three posts by drilling a series of holes close together, then routing them into one slot by slanting the bit. Post slots and bottoms were then treated with a wood preservative, allowed to dry and painted. After the posts were mounted over the brass deck anchors, holes were drilled through both posts and brass at one time to automatically line up the holes for the bolts. Ends of projecting bolts were hacksawed flush with nuts, filed smooth.

Step-by-step photos show exact method of construction, captions go into details. Briefly: back wall plate was installed first, notched to accept rafters after measuring overlapped Corrulux to find "centers." It was found that each 40-inch panel of Corrulux overlapped one corrugation, providing centers of 37⅜ inches. These centers dictate position of the rafters, one rafter under each overlap to provide a nailing surface. We preferred to use chrome-plated brass screws, these inserted through Neoprene washers to eliminate weather problems completely.

The cats—or short rafters—between the long, slanting beams, were cut to fit after long ones were installed for a perfect fit. These were simply toe-nailed into place. Rafters were also toe-nailed down to the front and top header plates. A one-foot pitch was decided upon to take care of drainage. This angle also went best with the rather shallow pitch of the shingled roof of our house.

With the framing complete, the entire wood structure was painted with silver paint. When this was dry, two coats of good outside white house paint were applied, allowing for drying in between. After this, of course, the Corrulux was installed and the covered patio was ready for use. Furniture, to go with our new outdoor living room, was picked to go with the clean, simple lines of the structure. The result was so pleasing that, except for extreme cold weather, we spend most of our free daytime hours outdoors. •

Metal-drilling bit is used to make a ⅜-inch hole through bottom of post, including hidden brass anchor plate, to receive a 5-inch stove bolt. If preferred, excess projection of bolt may be cut flush with nut after installation.

All rafters are now cut and placed on the headers. Back ends are inserted into the back plate slots, the front sections are placed over marked centers and toe-nailed into the front header plate. The inside front header is butted up against slanting rafters, and both plates fastened with stove bolts.

Patio Installation

An outdoor living room such as this one will contribute comfort and pleasure for years to come. Consider these materials and this design carefully

FEW projects rival the gratifying end result of an outside effort that provides you with the shelter and privacy of an outdoor living room. Here you can relax, the family can play, barbecues can be arranged, and with proper lighting and a fairly smooth concrete deck underfoot, you can have evening parties and dances—outdoors.

By using a modern material like Kaiser Aluminum Diamond-Rib panels, you can design a light, pleasant project that will please yourself and your neighbors. This is a good material for such a project since it can't fade and won't corrode, stain or rust. All you need do is hose it down occasionally.

The rib pattern makes it possible to use the material either vertically or horizontally. Or, for a different effect, you can in-

The conventional wire fence you can see in the background did no more than establish a boundary. Here, after preliminary planning, location stakes for the screen and cabana are being placed and strung out.

Rent a gas-driven digger. You can do in an hour what would normally take a day. Be sure to put a husky neighbor on the other side of the gas digger.

Posts should be set 18″ to 24″ into ground on top of a gravel lining; 4x4 redwood was used. Note dadoes for stringers have already been cut.

Stringers are installed next, using 16d galvanized nails. Toenail after placing in the dadoes with four nails angled from top and bottom.

stall alternate vertical and horizontal panels. Each sheet provides a four-foot-wide panel and you can get them in various lengths to suit the dimensions of your project. In this particular case we used 10-foot sheets, cut in half for 5-foot vertical installation. The panels we used on the roof were 16-footers, so we were able to get jointless installation except for the side laps.

You should start your project by giving careful consideration to layout. Most layouts provide protection from hot afternoon sun and privacy from the street side or the house next door.

The first part of the job is to set the posts. If your lot is level and you plan to butt the stringers, then your best bet is to dig the post holes to approximate depth and cut the post tops to a level line after they have been installed. This plan may also be fol-

lowed if the lot slopes, but if you plan on insetting the stringer ends in dadoes and don't object to a little, careful preplanning, you can save some trouble by precutting the posts to correct length and dadoing before installing them. Measure dado locations from the *top* of the posts; you can make some adjustments by altering the depth of the post-holes. A cleat, nailed to the post at the grade line, will maintain the correct post height until they are set.

We found it easier to place the posts in the holes and attach the stringers to get the entire framework assembled, before pouring concrete in the post holes. Braces, nailed to stakes driven in the ground, kept posts plumb until we were ready to pour.

If the roof will be part of the project, you can use extra long fence posts at that point to serve as verticals for the roof framing.

Use a level on two adjacent edges of the post before the stringers are installed. Temporary braces keep post plumb but recheck when stringing.

If you turn a corner, cut the stringer end at an angle to match, then trim off the projecting part. Curved board, right, outlines the patio.

Nail cleats to the posts at the grade line to maintain correct post height until the concrete has been mixed and poured into the post holes.

Beams which support the rafters for the aluminum rest on the post tops. You can be pretty flexible in design so long as the size of the beams you use are okay for the span involved. For example, if you were going to span 20 feet, you'd probably need a 4 x 12-in. beam. Not to support the light aluminum roof, of course, but so the beam itself wouldn't sag.

You can get free, expert information regarding your own particular situation merely by talking to your local building inspector. The average project of this type calls for 4x4 posts, 4x6 beams (or doubled 2x6s), and 2x6 rafters. Blocking or stretchers between rafters is 2x6 stock. The aluminum panels are nailed directly to this framework with special nails that have a weatherproof washer under their heads. •
——*R. J. De Cristoforo*

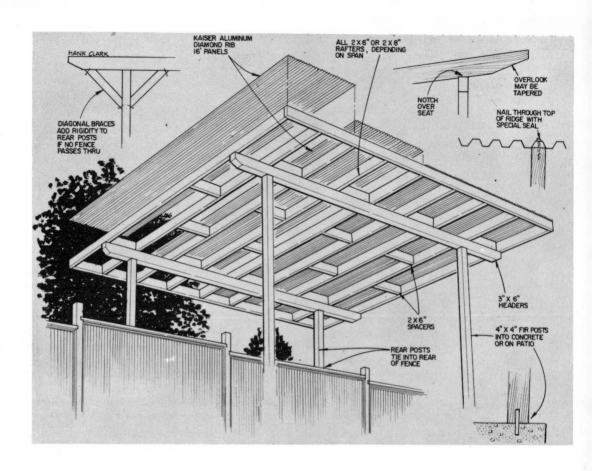

HANK CLARK

KAISER ALUMINUM
DIAMOND RIB
16' PANELS

ALL 2 X 6" OR 2 X 8"
RAFTERS, DEPENDING
ON SPAN

OVERLOOK
MAY BE
TAPERED

NOTCH
OVER
SEAT

NAIL THROUGH TOP
OF RIDGE WITH
SPECIAL SEAL

DIAGONAL BRACES
ADD RIGIDITY TO
REAR POSTS
IF NO FENCE
PASSES THRU

2 X 6"
SPACERS

3" X 6"
HEADERS

4" X 4" FIR POSTS
INTO CONCRETE
OR ON PATIO

REAR POSTS
TIE INTO REAR
OF FENCE

Kaiser aluminum sheets are cut with a power saw using a fine-tooth crosscut blade or flooring blade. Half a dozen sheets can be cut at once.

After painting fence frame, install sheets using cleat-framing. Cutting sheets ¼" shorter will facilitate installation; gap is covered by frame.

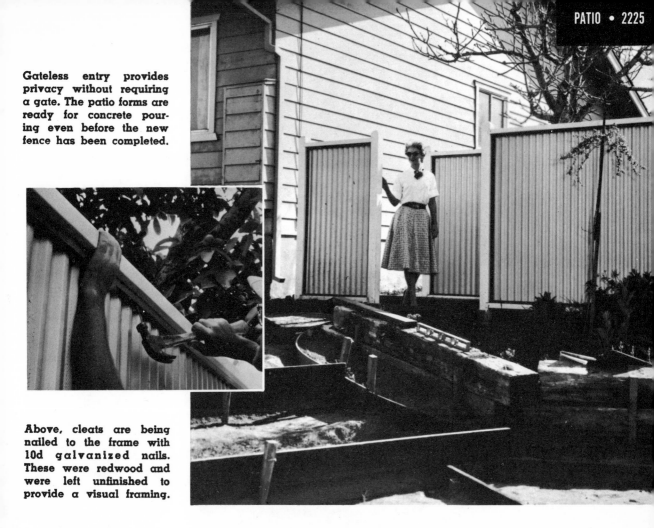

Gateless entry provides privacy without requiring a gate. The patio forms are ready for concrete pouring even before the new fence has been completed.

Above, cleats are being nailed to the frame with 10d galvanized nails. These were redwood and were left unfinished to provide a visual framing.

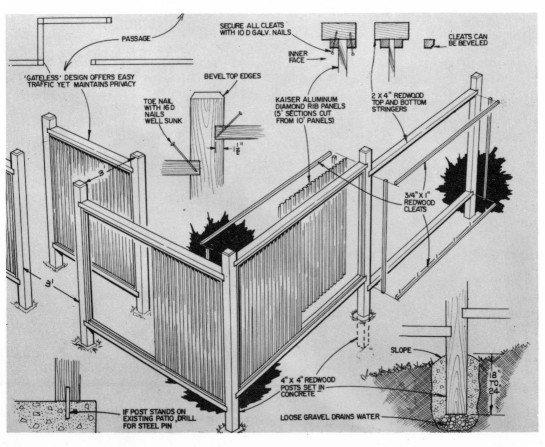

PASSAGE

SECURE ALL CLEATS WITH 10 D GALV. NAILS

INNER FACE

CLEATS CAN BE BEVELED

'GATELESS' DESIGN OFFERS EASY TRAFFIC YET MAINTAINS PRIVACY

BEVEL TOP EDGES

TOE NAIL WITH 16 D NAILS WELL SUNK

KAISER ALUMINUM DIAMOND RIB PANELS (5' SECTIONS CUT FROM 10' PANELS)

2 X 4" REDWOOD TOP AND BOTTOM STRINGERS

1½"

3/4" X 1" REDWOOD CLEATS

SLOPE

18 TO 24

IF POST STANDS ON EXISTING PATIO, DRILL FOR STEEL PIN

4" X 4" REDWOOD POSTS SET IN CONCRETE

LOOSE GRAVEL DRAINS WATER

Cover Your Patio

Patio covers of lightweight, colorful materials transform a simple concrete patio into a gracious outdoor living room

WHEN you move into your new home, chances are it will have a concrete patio—a good place for outdoor furniture and a barbecue. But you'll soon find that outdoor living is fun *except* when it rains or when the sun is too hot for anything but broiling. So one of your immediate needs is a patio cover to enable you to enjoy outdoor living.

Most times the cover material used is so light that it has no bearing on the framing material. That is, you don't have to bulk up the post, beams and rafters to support a great load. Usually the span of the supports (for example, distance between posts) determines the size of beams and rafters. Unless yours is a tremendous project in length and width, you'll be working with 2x4s, 2x6s and 4x4s.

Material Selection

Sometimes a patio cover is designed as an extension of the house roof in which case the cover material should probably match. But most often, even though attached to the house, the cover is a particular material, having characteristics that make it especially suitable for the purpose. It should be light, easy to handle, and require no excessive substructure. It should be translucent so the patio will be light. It should be workable with ordinary tools, and it should contribute to minimizing heat from the sun's rays. Most popular among materials that fill the bill are big, corrugated sheets of fiberglass.

Starting the Job

With the floor (concrete patio) already in, you can start the job by thinking about the posts (vertical members to support roof frame) and the header (a horizontal member attached to the house side of the patio). If the posts will rest directly on the concrete, you can use a ½" portable drill and a carbide-tipped bit to drill holes in the concrete. In the holes you cement ½-inch steel rods. Short lengths of concrete reinforcement steel will do. After you drill holes in the bottom of each post, set them over the projecting pins.

If you want a cover that extends beyond the concrete and the posts can't be set on the existing patio, you can excavate a hole

Start with a simple patio cover and eventually you can have an elaborate screened-in porch, as above. Here the roof and rear wall are made of Filon.

Patio, left, is enhanced by 2x6 grid frame on a 4x6 post supported by prefabricated wrought iron. The cover is made of corrugated Filon fiberglass.

Once you see your results you'll soon forget the time and effort you exerted in constructing your patio cover. Just try to think of all the years ahead of relaxing and fun-filled outdoor living!

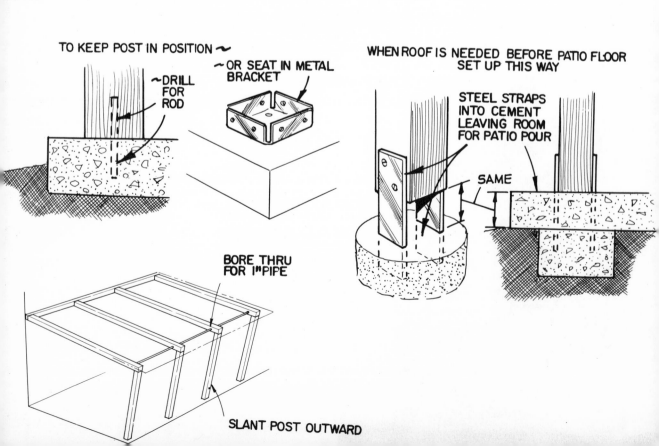

TO KEEP POST IN POSITION

~DRILL FOR ROD

~ OR SEAT IN METAL BRACKET

WHEN ROOF IS NEEDED BEFORE PATIO FLOOR SET UP THIS WAY

STEEL STRAPS INTO CEMENT LEAVING ROOM FOR PATIO POUR

SAME

BORE THRU FOR 1" PIPE

SLANT POST OUTWARD

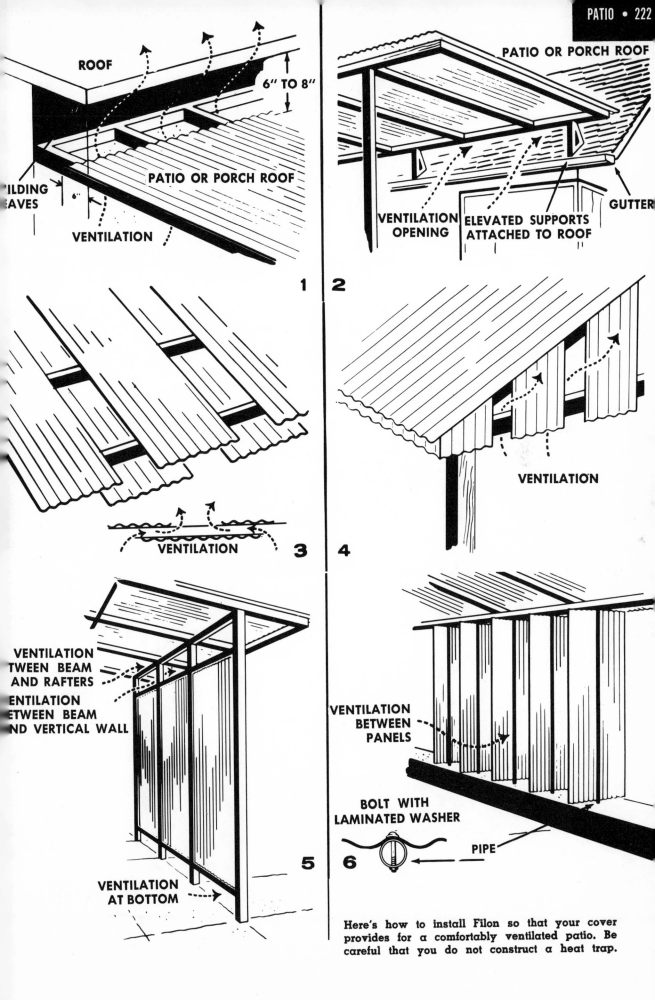

ROOF

6" TO 8"

PATIO OR PORCH ROOF

BUILDING EAVES

6"

VENTILATION

1

PATIO OR PORCH ROOF

VENTILATION OPENING

ELEVATED SUPPORTS ATTACHED TO ROOF

GUTTER

2

VENTILATION

3

VENTILATION

4

VENTILATION BETWEEN BEAM AND RAFTERS

VENTILATION BETWEEN BEAM AND VERTICAL WALL

VENTILATION AT BOTTOM

5

VENTILATION BETWEEN PANELS

BOLT WITH LAMINATED WASHER

PIPE

6

Here's how to install Filon so that your cover provides for a comfortably ventilated patio. Be careful that you do not construct a heat trap.

Before: This patio is merely a stark concrete floor with a couple of chairs—hardly inviting for all the hot summer afternoons ahead.

After: The same concrete floor, the same chairs—but now the patio is a cool haven for summertime relaxation, thanks to the Filon cover.

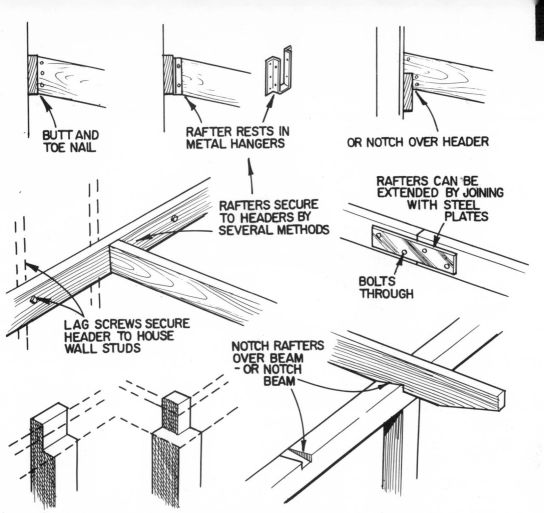

BUTT AND
TOE NAIL

RAFTER RESTS IN
METAL HANGERS

OR NOTCH OVER HEADER

RAFTERS SECURE
TO HEADERS BY
SEVERAL METHODS

RAFTERS CAN BE
EXTENDED BY JOINING
WITH STEEL
PLATES

BOLTS
THROUGH

LAG SCREWS SECURE
HEADER TO HOUSE
WALL STUDS

NOTCH RAFTERS
OVER BEAM
- OR NOTCH
BEAM

SEVERAL METHODS OF RESTING BEAMS OR RAFTERS ON POST TOPS

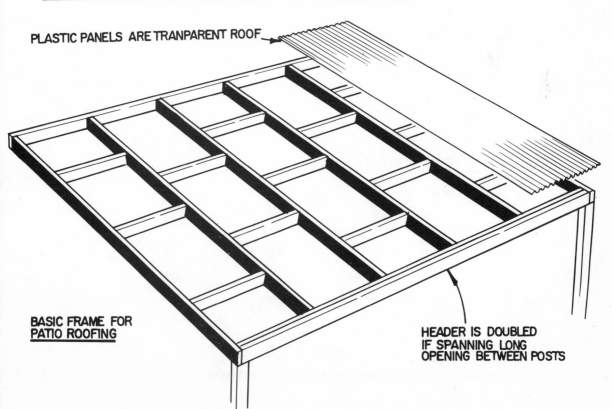

PLASTIC PANELS ARE TRANPARENT ROOF

BASIC FRAME FOR
PATIO ROOFING

HEADER IS DOUBLED
IF SPANNING LONG
OPENING BETWEEN POSTS

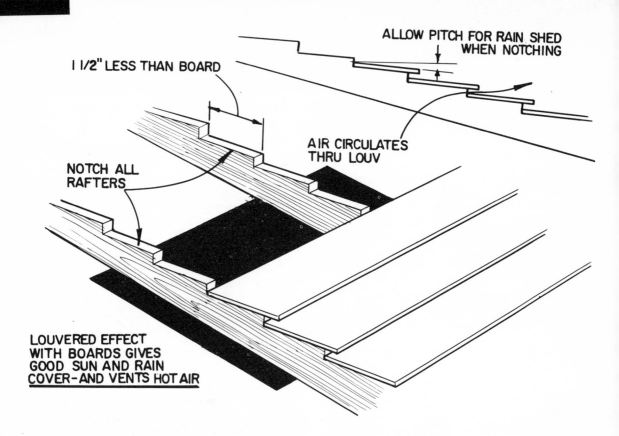

ALLOW PITCH FOR RAIN SHED WHEN NOTCHING

1 1/2" LESS THAN BOARD

AIR CIRCULATES THRU LOUV

NOTCH ALL RAFTERS

LOUVERED EFFECT WITH BOARDS GIVES GOOD SUN AND RAIN COVER—AND VENTS HOT AIR

Wrought iron is a favorite material to dress up a patio. To install the posts, drive the pins into expansion sleeves set in holes in the concrete.

Screw front header to post. Once rafters are strung from the house header to this one, the structure is rigid. Toenail header on wooden posts.

In this instance a lock joint was decided upon and made by notching both the header and the rafter. You can achieve the same results by using an alternative method—try toenailing the notched rafter.

The use of cross bracing not only provides support for the structure but also lends a decorative touch. Here cross braces create a lovely grid-like pattern.

Filon is very light and easy to lift. Cutting should be done on the ground with measurements carefully checked twice.

Always use special weatherproof nails with corrugated Filon. Drive the nails through peaks and never in the valleys.

This aluminum end-wall flashing prevents rain from seeping under the patio cover. It's just one of many accessories available for use with Filon. Flashing corrugations match those in fiberglass sheets. Use mastic very freely between the aluminum sheets and the walls of the house to prevent water seepage.

at each post location, set the post in the hole (after placing a two-inch layer of gravel) and then fill in with concrete.

The rafter at the house end is spiked directly to the house studs. If attaching to the house would make the patio cover too low at that end, or if it wouldn't provide adequate ventilation (see drawing), then you can put this member above the roof line on a series of adequate supports.

A second header is required across the posts. Unless the span is quite short, you'll need 6" stock—either two 2x6s or one 4x6. This can be toenailed at each post bearing point. Spanning across from the house header to the post header are the rafters. These can be butted at each end or they can rest on top of the supporting rafters. If you butt, consider the use of preformed metal hangers. These are very easy to install and cut out a lot of angle-nailing.

If you put the rafters on top of the supports, you should notch at the front end where they cross the post-header. The rafters do not have to end at the header. In fact, a nicer-looking job is always the result when the rafters extend beyond that point.

Cross bracing is added (especially if the material you use calls for it) by using stock that matches the rafter material. The braces can run in a line or they can be staggered to obtain a grid effect. The latter is preferable from a nailing standpoint since you can then nail through the rafter into the end of the brace.

If the framework requires painting do it now. It will be a lot easier at this point when you don't have to worry about splashing the cover material.

Fiberglass panels can be worked with a hand saw or a portable cut-off saw. Actual cutting can be minimized by the amount of preplanning you do. The fiberglass panels come in various lengths, so you can buy to the length you want. It's not too difficult to plan the width of the cover so as to use a certain number of panels without having to cut lengthwise. When figuring, be sure to include the overlap along the edges which is required for "drip-proof" construction.

The panels are nailed in place, but drill holes for the nails. Use nails at every second or third corrugation along the headers and space them 12 inches along headers and at cross braces. Special weatherproof nails with attached washers should be used. One wise precaution at overlaps is to lay down a bead of mastic between sheets and then nail to pull the sheets tightly at the mastic line. •

Paths, Patios

WITH the current emphasis on outdoor living, no home landscape is complete without an outdoor living room—a terrace or a patio. Also required are the hallways of your garden—paths or walks.

A major planning consideration is the function of the terrace or patio. If, for example, outdoor cooking and dining are contemplated, a barbecue of some sort must be included. If your outdoor living area is to be simply a cozy nook where you can relax and get some fresh air, you will want to take that into account.

The location of a patio is often determined by the placement of the house on the lot. If you have a choice in the matter,

In addition to concrete, flagstone, other materials, brick on sand makes attractive patios, paths. Put foundation layer of sand over cinders or gravel for good drainage, tamp it down as shown (right).

and Terraces

you might consider these things. First of all, it is often desirable to have a patio that is directly connected with an entrance to the house. This is especially helpful if the patio will be used for outdoor dining.

The location of the patio in relation to the sun is also a factor. If the outdoor living area faces east and is blocked on the west, for example, it will receive early morning sun and shade in the afternoon. This arrangement would work very well—especially if the patio also serves as a service area for clothes-drying. The area would be in the sunlight for hanging clothes in the morning and would be a source of relaxing shade in the afternoon. The reverse would be true where there is a western exposure.

A southern exposure receives sun all day long. In some sections of the North this arrangement might not be objectionable, but in the South it would be unbearably hot. A patio facing north, of course, receives full shade all day.

Just as the exposure tends to regulate the climate, it also regulates the plants you can grow successfully in the immediate

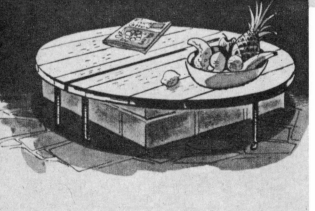

Bricks can be laid in attractive designs designs (r.). Brush sand in cracks to finish surface of brick patio. Hose sand down and repeat as necessary.

FURNISHING THE PATIO

If grass is to grow between flags, cut out sod, place stones, or spread soil in cracks, plant seed.

Whiting Photo

Galloway

Roofed-in barbecue highlights this attractive patio made of flagstones set in concrete.

vicinity. Where sun is limited, you must grow those plants that will endure a lack of sunshine. Where sun is plentiful, you have a wide range of sun—and heat—loving annuals for continuous color throughout the summer and into the fall.

What about the size of the patio? Try to look at the patio as another room of the house. It must be furnished and decorated like any other room. It will also have some permanent fixtures and a definite function. But unlike an inside room, you do have some control over its size and location.

For dining, and entertaining, a patio should be a fairly good size. If it's to be a restful nook, it may not need to be as large. Visualize the furnishings and barbecue—if you intend to have one—to help fix the size. You might use cardboard boxes to actually represent furnishings on the patio site.

While on the subject of a barbecue, check the prevailing breezes on the patio site. Many people have discovered—after finishing the job—that the wind drifts all the smoke from the barbecue into the sitting area.

MATERIALS: Solid concrete is a common patio construction material. Such an area is fine for tables and chairs, if you intend

Tatch

Interest is added to surface of concrete patio by inlaid pieces of redwood in a square pattern.

to entertain outdoors, and is also ideal for children and their tricycles.

A concrete patio can be dressed up with a design in the concrete. One possibility is to mark off lines to resemble those of ir- regular flagstones. A formal patio of con- crete can also be made more interesting by inserting strips of redwood 2 to 4 inches wide so the final job resembles a number of large blocks bordered by wood.

Concrete can also be painted to cut down the whiteness and make a smoother sur- face. It is possible to paint the irregular pattern of flagstone on concrete.

In addition to concrete, flagstone and brick can be used for patio construction. In

both cases, the material can be laid on a bed of sand. Sand is then brushed between the pieces to make a smooth surface.

The base layer of sand should be at least 2 inches thick and should be placed over a layer of cinders or gravel to give extra drainage.

To give the patio a firmness, soak the area with a hose after the stones or bricks are in place and the cracks filled. Most likely, another sweeping of sand will be needed between the bricks. After the sec- ond sweeping the patio floor should be firm. To keep weeds and grass from growing be- tween the bricks or flags, the area can be treated with a general or non-selective

Beautiful path with a gentle curve—flags with grass between—adds beauty but avoids extra walking.

weed killer. One application is about all that will be needed to last a full season.

Decorations complete your outdoor living area. Low walls can be added at patio boundaries and planted with either annuals or perennials. Roses are the choice of many for patio decoration. These can be planted in wooden tubs or planters and moved about just as you move furniture.

Several trees may be needed to furnish a roof of shade in locations where sun shines hot for long hours. Since it will take time for trees to grow, a temporary cover or awning will be needed. A constructed roof can also be installed. Some elaborate patios even have screened sides for complete protection from insects.

TERRACING: It is often desirable to have a gentle slope to a lawn, but when a patio is constructed, a flat space must be provided. A situation of this sort calls for terracing. When you have a patio that overlooks a garden—often a very attractive arrangement—it can truly be called a terrace rather than a patio.

There is an art in building retaining walls for terrace. Unless they are correctly constructed, the results can be unsightly and may eventually collapse.

It is important to remember that just a few feet of soil will exert a pressure measured in tons. The wall must be strong enough to bear a good part of the weight. Since more pressure is exerted at the base than at the top, a retaining wall should be wider at the bottom. As a precaution, whether the retaining wall will be a strong mortared one or just a dry wall, there should be a sturdy footing of poured concrete that reaches below the frost level.

If the wall is to be masonry with mortared cement blocks, bricks or field stones, it can be constructed in the conventional manner. Again, however, it would be a good idea to make it thicker at the base than at the top.

Take extra precautions with a dry stone wall. Structures of this type should always be considerably thicker at the base. Next, and most important, there should be a slant to the stones down and into the wall. If

Terrace wall above embodies correct construction technique, extends well below the frost level.

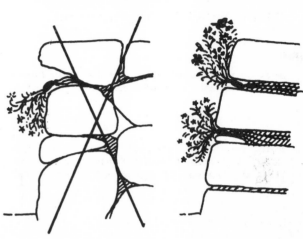

Retaining wall at edge of sloping lawn is shown above, right. The decorative plants add interest.

Right, wrong construction is shown at right. Slope wall inward, make it wider at base than at top.

Surface of a retaining wall also offers decorating opportunities. Plant in between the stones.

this is not done, there will be a flow of water and soil out from between the stones following a heavy rain.

Once these considerations are taken care of, there is no drainage problem with a dry wall. With a solid wall there sometimes is. The extra pressure exerted by flowing water pushes on the wall and, in the event of a heavy rainfall, could even collapse it if drainage is not provided. Leave drainage holes along the base of the wall.

Adequate drainage is important for another reason. Even a small amount of water trapped behind a solid wall will make the upper terrace pretty soggy and damp. It could affect the patio floor on top and will, of course, play havoc with the plants and lawn.

Instead of using a wall, the terracing could be done with a slope. This will take up more room than a narrow wall, but will give you the opportunity of adding a rock garden and other interesting vines and ground covers. Don't make the slope too steep or you will be troubled with wash-outs. On the other hand, the slope should not be too wide. You want to be able to care for the plants without being a mountain climber.

Wherever possible, use plants to provide a touch of color to your terrace wall. With the proper plants added—on top or within the wall—it can become the most interesting and beautiful feature in your landscape.

GARDEN PATHS: In every garden there is a need for a walk or path. The basic function of a path is to provide a convenient way of getting from one place to another. A garden walk, however, should be esthetically pleasing while contributing to the landscape.

A straight line is the shortest distance between two points, but in many landscapes, a straight line doesn't conform, or add, to the general layout. A straight walk may even detract from the general appearance of the grounds.

Unless yours is a strictly formal garden, you should strive for gently curving paths and walks. This doesn't mean that you

Brick on sand paths, walks, can be either formal or informal, and elaborate or simple in design.

Rustic path of field stone is adequate for light traffic, is in keeping with the rural surroundings. Stone is "planted" by cutting out pieces of sod.

should greatly increase the length of the path or double back over ground already covered. Try to picture the walk as a straight line and then gently curve it so that in essence you are still providing a useful roadway between two points.

Construction of individual walks and paths will depend on the use they receive. The main walk from the street to the house must be well built and wide enough for at least two people walking abreast. On the other hand, a back path leading to another portion of the garden which is used only during the summer months and then only a few times a week, can be more on the ar-

tistic side rather than utilitarian. This path, too, will rarely be cleared of snow and can be a part of the garden. In this instance, a few plants or grass growing between the stones may be desirable whereas on the front walk it would not be.

ATTRACTIVE STEPS can be used to complete the garden when the property is hilly or located on a slope. Among the things that can be used to construct steps are—in addition to poured concrete—railroad ties, timbers, tiles, logs, bricks, concrete blocks, cut stone and field stone.

When the path goes from one level to another, there is a need for steps. Wide steps are preferable if two or more people will be using the walk at the same time. The rise of garden steps does not have to conform with the usual ones found in most stairways, but the steps should be comfortable to walk on. If the rise is too low, people may trip on the steps; if too tall, you will have to jump up.

The depth of the steps can be greater than usual. You can design them so that the user takes two full strides rather than one. In all cases, however, try to use a size that will not necessitate a breaking of your stride when you climb the steps. Remember the overhang of the steps, too. People need this area for their toes.

Steps can be made of any suitable material. When using stone such as flags or brick, the steps should be layed firmly on a concrete base. A sand base will do for path and patio but when it comes to steps you need something firm. Otherwise, you will be repairing steps every year. Be sure, too, that the footing of the concrete base is below frost line. •

Gravel, crushed stone and bluestone make good paths—will take a considerable amount of traffic.

Simple but effective garden steps leading to an upper terrace are constructed of railroad ties.

sectional

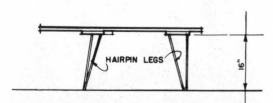

ELEVATION

USE 3/4" PLYWOOD EXTERIOR A-C
GLUE (WATERPROOF) PLY. PADS AND
NAIL WITH 6d FINISH NAILS.

HAIRPIN LEGS

16"

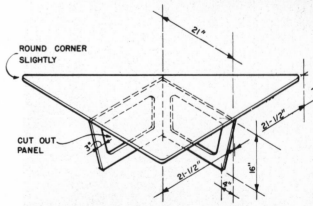

ROUND CORNER
SLIGHTLY

CUT OUT
PANEL

21"

21-1/2"

21-1/2"

16"

3"

4"

ALTERNATE DESIGN USING PLYWOOD LEGS

patio tables

Their unconventional shape makes for interesting arrangements

INTERESTING arrangements of these triangular tables are a natural result of their unconventional shape. Group two or more in various ways, or tuck only one in a hard-to-fit corner. Painted in brilliant, contrasting primary colors, they can brighten a terrace in fascinating ways. Construction is the ultimate in simplicity. The inexpensive hairpin legs shown are available everywhere and easy to install. Use only Exterior type fir plywood made with 100% waterproof glue and durable, high quality exterior paint or enamel.

Several tables can be stored in an out-of-the-way corner during the winter, as they can be stacked top up and top down, one above the other. But the chances are that you'll want to use them indoors, too, once you build them.

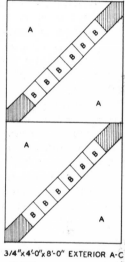

3/4"x4'-0"x8'-0" EXTERIOR A-C
CUTTING DIAGRAM
(4 PATIO TABLES)

PARTS SCHEDULE FOR TWO PATIO TABLES

CODE	NO. REQ'D	SIZE	PART IDENTIFICATION
A	2	43" x 43"	Top of Tables
B	6	7" x 7"	Pads for Legs
	6 ea.	3/8" Diam.	Wrought Iron Legs

MISCELLANEOUS: Waterproof Glue
Screws as Required

PLAN

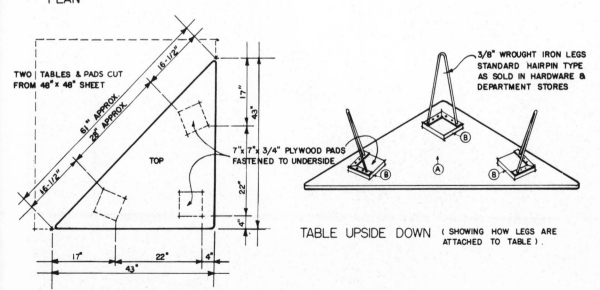

TWO TABLES & PADS CUT FROM 48" x 48" SHEET

16-1/2"

61" APPROX.
28" APPROX.

16-1/2"

TOP

7"x 7"x 3/4" PLYWOOD PADS FASTENED TO UNDERSIDE

17"

43"

22"

4"

17"   22"   4"

43"

3/8" WROUGHT IRON LEGS STANDARD HAIRPIN TYPE AS SOLD IN HARDWARE & DEPARTMENT STORES

TABLE UPSIDE DOWN (SHOWING HOW LEGS ARE ATTACHED TO TABLE).

The Wide World of Patio Gardening

by Jack Kramer

Exotic plants can now create a tropical paradise in your own back yard.

PATIOS and outdoor living areas are now an aspect of our way of life even where summers are short. The new concept of architecture using large spans of glass and organic materials make it necessary for us to soften the stark concept with living plants. Thus, a balance between indoors and outdoors is created, harmony developed and beauty the result. Ten years ago it was impossible to obtain large exotic plants; today, it is a matter of overnight transportation. Jet planes, new insecticides have given us the opportunity to beautify our new homes, indoors and out. Hundreds of new plants are available. As we move ahead in unrelated fields we also progress in the plant world.

The plants we have known in the past simply do not furnish the decorative ac-cent necessary for large terraces, atriums, and patios. Hoyas and ferns are too small, better at the window than outdoors. We need large dramatic plants; we know how to grow them, suppliers finally know how to crate them and ship them. The changing shadows of foliage, the dramatic color of bloom, the pleasing evening scents are what make the difference between an outdoor area seldom used and one that is always in use. We desire motion and design. Living plants fulfill this void.

The type of outdoor area dictates what kind of plant to have. If it is a protected structure (with roof) it is suitable for certain plants. If the area is open to weather, other tropical plants will do better. The climate you live in plays a role in the plants you select. The purpose of this book is to

Collecting epiphytes from trees. Plants are flown to nurseries that specialize in tropical plants.

Paul C. Hutchison

Architectural Pottery

Succulents in containers on patio floor. A variety of containers is available.

furnish information about plants that can successfully grow in your own individual outdoor area whether it be a patio or terrace, an atrium or solarium or simply an open porch.

WHERE THEY COME FROM

Patio plants come from all over the world and they can be as colorful for us in our outdoor living areas as they are in their native lands. While it is true that some of them grow in tropical humid forests, the majority of them inhabit regions where there are cool nights. Plants are not as fragile as we might think. With proper care, they can be grown successfully on patio or atrium.

Knowing where a plant comes from is a great help in determining what kind of culture it should have. If it is from Brazil or Central America where there is a dry and a rainy season we know that the plant must rest at some time of the year. If it is from Ceylon or New Guinea where there are no defined seasons—this indicates the plant will grow all year.

There are many new plants for patios and terraces now available for the first time. Jet air cargo—overnight shipment, new insecticides that do not kill plants at port of entry—make it possible for us to have a wide selection of plant material to decorate patios. Glamorous ginger plants and floriferous orchids can now become part of daily living. Bromeliads from South America have finally made their appearance in our country; you cannot find a better patio plant.

Paul C. Hutchison

Orchids clinging to the side of a mountain in Peru. Thousands of plants grow at different levels here.

These decorative plants grow at varying levels in their native lands. Generally, at 2000 feet the climate would be between 55 and 90 degrees and here philodendron, begonias, ginger and orchids thrive. While many are on the forest floor where it may be warm day and night, for every 1000 feet the temperature drops 5 degrees. Since the majority of plants grow at 2000 to 6000 feet, they are quite accustomed to cool evenings. On mountain slopes of Central America at 4000 feet where it is moist and cool we find achimenes, anthuriums and ferns. The western coast of South America —Chile, Peru, Ecuador and Colombia—is mountainous; thousands of plants grow at different levels here. At 6000 feet with a temperature of 48 degrees. Cattleya orchids thrive. At 13,000 feet in Peru, Stenia orchids flourish.

WHERE TO BUY THEM

Rather than importing your own plants (although this is possible) it is best to buy them from nurseries that specialize in tropical plants. They bring the plants into the country and establish them (grow them on for several months) so the risky time of adjustment is over when you get them.

These nurseries are located in all parts of our country. Some are in the East, the West, the Midwest and many in the South.

Some nurseries are better for certain plants than others. It is quite simple; the owner is fond of a specific plant group and grows them to perfection. Others specialize in orchids or bromeliads and still others offer the best selection of foliage plants. Before ordering plants it is best to write for catalogs and listings. This will tell you what kind of supplier you are dealing with.

Once you find a good source for a certain group of plants, it is best to buy from them.

Since a great many patio plants are large (7 feet or more) shipping must be done carefully. It is best to have the plants arrive in pots rather than to have them uprooted and shipped bare root. They will have to adjust to new conditions with you. That is enough of a problem at the start. Later, they can be transplanted. If you are fortunate, the plants will be in plastic pots and shipping is not too costly. However, many times they are in oil cans which are unsightly and expensive to transport. Still, through the years I have found it better to leave them in their containers and re-

pot them later after they have adjusted to their new surroundings. Smaller plants, most times, can be shipped bare root if you desire it. They adjust easily.

Whether you order the plants bare root or in pots, tell the supplier they must be in ventilated boxes and wrapped in paper or other protective coating. Further, instruct him to put your phone number on the carton, so railway express and air offices will not detain the plants. I have used this method with tremendous success. I am called immediately and usually pick up the plants myself. I have had tropical plants, 8 feet tall, shipped from Florida and New Jersey and other parts of the country that arrived in perfect condition in California.

If the pots are not anchored with staples or rope to the bottom of the container, they may arrive broken. Do not refuse the shipment; it is a simple matter to repot the plants. However, notify the supplier that in the future you want all pots secured properly. Unwrap the plants carefully; you yourself can damage them by pulling and tearing the paper.

When on vacation stop at the nurseries

A lush banana plant in the jungle is shown, left.
Paul C. Hutchison

Clay pots, tools, cold frames, in compact area.

Clay-potted plants displayed in pyramid off this semishaded shelter of California redwood slats.

and select your plants for future shipment. Not only will you receive what you want but you will enjoy the visit too. Most nurseries are splendid display places to linger on an afternoon. Of course, if you have local nurseries, search for your own plants. And do some greenhouse hunting in your city. You will be amazed at what you can find if you know what you are looking for. A night blooming cactus, an exotic ficus tree, a Christmas cactus have been my reward on several occasions.

METHODS OF SHIPPING

If at all possible, ship your plants Air Parcel Post. This method usually gets them to you the next day. Sometimes it is necessary to pick them up at the airport but it is not a complicated procedure. Railway Express is another way to ship plants. However, although cheaper than air over a long distance, it takes too much time and it is wiser to invest extra money in Air Parcel Post. Shipping by Greyhound Bus is excellent for short distances, but in most cases you will have to pick up the plants. Regular Parcel Post is fine for small shipments.

Sometimes if you are having many plants shipped, as I do, it is best to specify two medium size crates to one very large one. Usually the supplier is cognizant of shipping regulations (size of box, united inches), but it does no harm to request exactly what you want. Check on your end with railway and air offices to find out if there are any restrictions as to size and type of boxes. Also check with the shipper —air or railway—to see if the plants have arrived. Plants shipped collect usually get faster service.

Spring and fall are the best times to ship plants. In the winter, weather is too risky and in the summer I have found more plants succumb to heat than to zero weather. •

Paul C. Hutchison

Orchids, above, growing on tree in rain forest.

Strawberry plants; inverted clay pots for height.

Bromeliads growing on tree in South America.
Paul C. Hutchison

Molly Adams

A small patio of lawn and brick. An intimate and cozy place for morning coffee, afternoon chats

The Patio

Well planned and carefully planted, your patio can
enhance the comfort and value of your home.

A PATIO can be many things—a place by the garden, an enclosed court, a terrace alongside the house, an outdoor recreation room. No matter what we call it, a patio is essentially an outdoor room. Shrubs and trees are the walls, grass or brick the carpeting and the sky, the ceiling.

The word patio is basically Spanish meaning a court of a house. The patio garden most probably developed from the Roman atrium. The Spanish climate was warm and sunny and houses were built with open patios or courtyards. These areas were decorated with lavish detail— iron grilles, stonework and filled with all types of plants. Originally, the patio was always a part of the house and enclosed on four sides to bring into the rooms a garden atmosphere. Now, although we frequently see the patio in the guise of an atrium with the house around it, it is most often in the rear open to the landscape and adjoining a living room or dining room.

SIZE

Most patios are in back of the house where there is space and privacy and seclusion from the street. Front patios between the house and street are possible but take careful planning to overcome the difficulties. It is not fully private and constructing a fence as a barrier is often costly.

A patio alongside a house is possible if there is enough space. Generally, city lots are narrow and, too, neighbors' windows may adjoin the area. However, successful side-yard patios have been built with tall hedges or fences to assure privacy.

The patio should be in scale with the

Foliage plants in patio area with protective roof lathing.

Formal patio with large area of seemingly natural plantings.
Nat. Concrete Masonry Assoc.

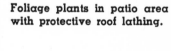

Even a back yard in the city can take on the aspects of a comfortable patio. Note clay-potted plants.

house. While it is nice to have a large area we must remember that the outdoor room when furnished and with living plants becomes an integral part of the home. Balance must be created and unity established. A too-large patio is bleak and uninviting. If the lot size is large and calls for a big expanse, break it up into separate terraces and patios. Remember that a patio is a steppingstone to the outdoors.

The size of the house and the surrounding land and shrubbery determine the size of the patio. If there are large trees and shrubs around the location it becomes necessary to have a patio that balances the grand scale of the outdoors. If, on the other hand there is a small garden and little space, an intimate patio is more charming.

There must be unity to the patio and its surroundings, too. A visual balance between trees and shrubs and container plants on the patio must be created. And mass and color must be worked out in pleasing proportions.

LOCATION

Sun and wind must be taken into consideration when building a patio. A patio facing south will have harsh sunlight most of the year. In summer, noon rays will burn plants. There are all kinds of movable canopies and lath roofings to help shield

Classic open porch becomes patio area with proper furniture, plants. Molla, Inc.

Indoor-outdoor patio room is accomplished with plants, glass walls. American Furniture Mart

Roofless outdoor dining nook made with redwood walls, clay pots, etc.

Potted plants can turn room with sliding glass doors into "patio area."

Potted geraniums, planters of annuals enhance swimming pool area.

Nat. Concrete Masonry Assoc.

Molla, Inc.

Patio for entertaining
with specimen tree,
wall and boxed plants.

Nat. Concrete Masonry Assoc.

Entrance to patio is dramatized with clay-potted petunias and geraniums.

Informal but functional
patio area is planted
well, provides privacy.
Furniture Mart

Circular patio has good,
natural background. Add
potted plants as shown.
Nat. Concrete Masonry Assoc.

Nat. Concrete Masonry Assoc.

This circular patio follows contours of landscape, makes full use of natural, existing trees, shrubs.

and protect plants and still be a pleasing part of the outdoor area. Wind can be an enemy, too; it rips leaves and knocks over plants. A brick or stone wall on the east or west exposure may be desirable. With espalier plants, barriers become attractive.

A west patio can become unbearably hot in the afternoon. Without overhead protection too much heat is radiated and it is a place to avoid rather than spend leisure hours. Overhead roofing, with vines perhaps, or tall shrubbery help remedy the problem.

A patio that faces east is warmed by the morning sun and cools off in the afternoon. Overhead protection is not necessary and the area can be a pleasant retreat. Plants grow exceptionally well in this exposure benefitting from morning sun and protected

from building heat of the afternoon sun.

While it is possible to have a terrace or patio on the north side of the house it is not desirable. Although there are shade-growing plants, the majority of species must have scattered sunlight. North areas, for the most part, should be small and charming rather than full-scale patios.

A patio can be for people—a place to have morning coffee or lunch—furnished with wicker or rattan pieces. Or it can be a place primarily for plants; a lush green jungle to stroll at leisure. A patio can also be a place for the barbecue and a place for the children to play. And, of course, it can be a combination of all three things if space is available.

Decide what you want it to be before you start to plan it; it saves a great deal of work later. •

Credit: Architectural Pottery

Sizes and shapes of containers are important not only for design but for ample root growth area.

The Containers

Formula for patio beauty: The right plant, the right spot, the right pot.

City terrace is embellished with French umbrella, wall and clay-potted plantings.

Hanging containers put plants at eye level where they get light, be fully appreciated.

TODAY, there is an unlimited variety of containers sold. Choice becomes vital. Some plants are airy, vertical and demand a certain kind of container, others are bushy and need different kinds of pots. We want a patio or terrace that is pleasing in all aspects—plants, pots, setting. Containers become part of the furnishings. What looks good in one pot will not necessarily be handsome in another container. The right plant in the right pot placed in a proper spot give the unity and balance needed to make a patio beautiful.

POTS AND TUBS

The standard clay pot was one of the

Soy tubs, ideal containers, come in many sizes.   Cylinder type pots are decorative patio planters.

Clay pots and simple box for plantings bring a touch of the country to this city back yard patio.

Hanging baskets of Coleus lend a soft and natural touch to the harsh mechanics of patio canopy.

Random hanging pots, baskets and decorations lend the mood you desire to the entrance of your patio.

Architectural Pottery photo, left, shows how pot design can complement and enhance overall patio design. Textured wooden baskets, above, can be utilized for general use or for hanging plants.

earliest containers to be used. Today they range in size from 3 to 24 inches in diameter. They are easy to use, inexpensive and the natural clay color harmonizes with outdoor settings. Recently, many variations of the standard pot have appeared at nurseries. The Italian pot modifies the border to a tight-lipped detail, simple and good looking. Some have rounded edges, others are beveled or rimless. Size: 12 to 26 inches.

The azalea pot, a squatty clay container formerly sold in only a few sizes is now available from 6 to 14 inches in diameter. Three-legged clay pots are new, bring the bowl shape to the patio. Sizes: 8 to 20 inches in diameter.

Although the unglazed pot is most popular, glazed pots in many colors are attractive, too. These are frequently without drainage holes so watering must be done carefully. Waterlogged soil kills plants. All new pots, glazed or unglazed should be soaked overnight before they are used. Otherwise, they absorb the water from the soil needed by the plant. This is important.

Clay pots are satisfactory for small plants, wooden tubs are better for large plantings because they are not as heavy and have insulation value. Even in hot sun, heat penetrates wood slowly and roots are not liable to be scorched.

Stone or concrete tubs are ornamental, add dimension to a patio and are perfect for perennials. Shallow tapered bowls are especially pretty filled with petunias and marigolds. At the end of a terrace wall or at eye level they are dramatic.

Japanese soy tubs are inexpensive, handsome on the patio and plants look good in them. They are at nurseries and basket shops. Wood and bamboo tubs with large foliage plants are also effective outdoors. Galvanized washtubs, painted, with holes punched in the bottom for drainage filled with geraniums or heliotrope can be an eye-stopping display on the patio. Sawed-off wine casks, barrels and kegs are other container ideas. They are unique, add accent to the outdoor living room.

BOXES AND PLANTERS

Trees and large shrubs demand wooden boxes. The largest tub does not hold enough soil or carry enough visual weight to balance a tree. Some boxes are a perfect cube, others a low cube. In most cases the simple box is fine. However, they can become something more than a box with a little handiwork. Once you have the basic container there is much that can be done to vary its design: Nail 1 x 1-inch woodstrips spaced ½ inch apart around the box. Use wooden corners and 1 x 3-inch stock for a cap molding. Nail ½ x 1-inch lath spaced ½ inch apart vertically on the box. For a large box in a prominent spot place heavy trim around it; use 2 x 2 lumber.

There are a number of variations for boxes; let your imagination ramble. Dress them up; it takes but a few minutes. Put the right tree or shrub in an attractive detailed container and you have real accent for the patio.

A large box with a potted tree weighs several hundred pounds. If you are not in

Sheltered patio area is perfect spot for outdoor breakfasts. Note clay-potted plants, art objects.

Baskets of fuchsias in the rear of the area frame this "dining room" patio.

Conversation area is enhanced by addition of hanging fuchsia baskets.

Cylindrical ceramic pots for patio planting come in various textures and sizes.

Large Aralia plant, bottom left, finds a large redwood pot is a suitable container.

Windmill plants in decorated cylindrical pots; excellent complement to wood steps.

Credit: Architectural Pottery

Young succulents in architectural containers decorate a high wall off wood-decked patio entrance.

all year temperate climate you will have to store the tree over winter. Buy the commercial dollies with wheels and put them under the boxes so they can be moved about easily.

Planters can be freestanding or permanent of any given design—triangular, oblong or rectangular. Used for patio borders or grouped in corners they do much to make patio gardening instant gardening. With geraniums and agapanthus the patio becomes colorful in one afternoon. Portable wooden units can be rearranged at any time. Put them where you think they look the best. They can be window box size, 30 x 60 or perhaps just a small box 12 inches square, 8 inches deep for spring bulbs. They are at nurseries or you can easily make your own planters. Use 1-inch redwood stock for boxes less than 18 inches, 2-inch stock for larger ones. Nail the ends securely or use screws. Put 1 x 3-inch cleats across the bottom to keep the box off the ground. Bore ½-inch holes in the bottom of the container for drainage.

Permanent planters for the patio can be made of various materials—brick, fieldstone, flag strip, or concrete blocks. Choose the type that best complements your home. For a masonry planter, dig a trench 6 to

New "rimless" clay pots, above, make neat containers for plantings.
Succulents, left, in an Architectural Pottery accent floor container.
The popular Jade Plant in attractive three-legged clay pot, below.

A lacy Pittisporum in a water cooler container.

Camellia in home-made wooden container on base.

Author's photo

Schefflera growing in barrel in patio entrance.

Selection of wooden tubs and planters for patio.

Architectural Pottery containing Dracaena plants in interesting treatment, above.

20 inches deep, making it 3 to 4 inches wider than the masonry wall you are planting. Fill with concrete to serve as a foundation. Dig to local frost line which will vary from area to area. When footing is dry lay stone or brick on. it to desired shape. When walls have reached desired height trim it with a concrete cap.

HANGING BASKETS

Hanging containers in the patio suspended from eaves or rafters put plants in an enviable position to enjoy light and put foliage and blossoms at eye level where they can be fully appreciated. To-

day, all kinds of hanging baskets are at nurseries and florist shops. There are wooden ones, wire ones, plastic kinds and also clay types. There are also one-of-a-kind containers from ceramists.

The open-slatted redwood basket commonly used for orchids is a good one to work with. They look something like an inverted, tapered log cabin and allow sufficient circulation of air without rapid loss of moisture by evaporation through slatted sides. Conventional wire baskets are good too. They are inexpensive, lightweight; possibly the best containers. Line them with sphagnum moss or asmunda and fill

Hexagonal planters contain clay pots, change with seasons. Architectural Pottery, right, for accent.

Decorative pots go well with large accent plants.

with mix. Most baskets come with wire, chain, or rope for hanging. Simply put a screw eye or a clothesline hook into the ceiling or rafter edge and the plant is ready for hanging.

Where you hang the basket depends largely on what you have to hang them on or from. The outer periphery of the patio is good—there are rafters or beams, places to put the baskets. There are also wall brackets with adjustable arms.

It is well to remember that plants hung too far above eye level are not easily seen and they must not be in the way of room traffic. Being forced to duck around a plant is bothersome. So put hanging baskets in suitable places where they do not interfere with people and so that they are at proper eye level to give maximum effect. A stepladder or stepstool is almost essential when you water basket plants, or at least a long-beaked watering can. •

Large Specimen Plants

Potted trees or large shrubs are necessary to balance your outdoor decor.

Foliage plants along the house wall and a large specimen Monstera deliciosa decorate this patio.
Bethlehem Steel Co.

NEARLY every homeowner longs for trees and shrubs to complement his house and balance the landscape. Patios simply are not furnished without these plants. And potted trees and shrubs can be yours without waiting years for them. They are available at nurseries; select them carefully for your given area.

Called specimen plants, large trees and shrubs cost from $10.00 to $100.00. If your patio is hot and sunny, you might want a big leafy kind for shade. If the area is shady you might want the lacy design of a *Ficus Benjamina.*

The relationship between the tree and its tub must be considered. A 4-foot tree would be maximum for a 24-inch tub. This gives a satisfying balance and the container remains subordinate. Square or rectangular boxes always seem the best for trees with bold foliage. Lacy leaved trees like Japanese maples look best in tubs.

A container tree is heavy; be sure it can be moved easily. Small commercial dollies with casters are sold at nurseries or make your own device. All you need is a heavy piece of plywood and some 2-inch casters.

Trees are available in five gallon or in fifteen gallon size or in large boxes.

TREES

Acer palmatum, the Japanese maple is a lovely slow growing tree with lacy leaves.

It is handsome in soy tubs or redwood containers. Needs protection from sun and direct wind. Hardy to 0 degrees.

Datura candida known as Angel's Trumpet is a small tree with large white flowers. The leaves are grayish green, thick and velvety. Needs sun, protection from wind. Hardy to 30 degrees.

Eriobotrya japonica, the Loquat is a round headed tree with leathery dark green leaves. Excellent for tub or box on patio. Hardy to 20 degrees.

Ficus benjamina is a lovely small tree with tiny dark green leaves; branches have sculptural quality. Tree takes abuse and still grows well. Tender.

Ficus retusa, Indian Laurel Fig is popular, fast growing. With dense dark green foliage it is an attractive tub plant. Hardy to 30 degrees.

Lagerstroemia indica, Crepe Myrtle. A deciduous slow growing tree with crinkled pink flowers like cockscombs. Needs full sun and summer warmth. Tender.

Laurus nobilis, Grecian Laurel; a compact tree with broad base, often several trunks to a tree. Slow growing with dark evergreen foliage. Hardy to 20 degrees.

Pinus mugo mughas, Mugho pine is shrubby and spreading. Good for redwood tubs. Hardy.

Palms. Many good ones. (*Phoenix loureiri*) is a slow growing, dwarf with arch-

Aralias are a lush, dark green. They grow well as patio plants providing a thick, interesting mass.

ing fronds. (*Howea forsteriana*) is also good and the Lady Palm (Raphis excelsa) shrubby and graceful. Hardy to 25 degrees.

Magnolia grandiflora, the Southern Magnolia, has dark green glossy leaves, brown on undersides. Large white flowers in summer. Slow growing, good in any container. Hardy to 15 degrees. One of the best.

Schefflera acontifolia, the Australian Umbrella Tree, has graceful stems tipped with fronds of leaves. It takes abuse and still survives. Hardy to 30 degrees.

Flowering cherry and flowering apricot are also excellent as container trees for patios. Citrus—lemon, orange and grapefruit are other ideas.

SHRUBS

Abutilon, the Flowering Maple, has bell shaped flowers in many colors from yellow and orange to red. Amenable plants, they need plenty of water, some sunlight.

Camellia japonica, a splendid container plant, bears a profusion of flowers. Many varieties grown, all make a striking patio display. Most varieties need bright light, plenty of water and feeding. Hardy to 15 degrees.

Carissa grandiflora, an evergreen shrub, grows to about five feet. It has white flowers and red plumfruit. Nice growth habit; another good one. Hardy to 26 degrees.

Hibiscus rosa-sinensis, the Chinese hibiscus, grow to about six feet. It has dark glossy green foliage, flowers single or double, many colors offered. Hibiscus need sunlight and buckets of water. Hardy to 40°. Stunning accent.

Gardenia jasminoides, a lush shrub with dark green leaves and fragrant white blooms, does well in tubs. It is best to keep the soil somewhat dry rather than soggy wet. Shrub is hardy to 20 degrees.

Ilex aquifolium, English Holly is the traditional Christmas holly. It grows to about 8 feet in tubs. Blooms in May followed by red berries. Hardy to 15 degrees.

Ixora is an overlooked plant, and yet there are many varieties available that are very floriferous and the blooms come in a wide range of colors. There are brilliant yellows and whites and many shades of orange. These are good evergreen shrubs that stay in color a long time. Need sun, plenty of water. Grow indoors at a sunny window in winter.

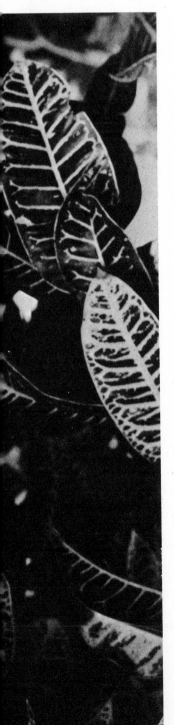

Crotons, left, have red foliage, are inexpensive and colorful.
Author's photo

Foliage plants neatly round off a dull corner of the patio.

A small Mahonia in a soy tub becomes focal point of patio.
Author's photo

Brick planter with ferns, fuchsia, and succulents.

Another of the Dieffenbachias for foliage accent, at right.

This photo shows how the root ball of large plants is wrapped in burlap at the nursery.

Holly shrub has dark green foliage, red berries.　　Small tree Podocarpus perfect in patio corner.

The popular rubber tree is a good foliage plant.

Jatropha Pandurifolia has clusters of red flowers blooming over a long season. Needs bright light rather than sun, lots of water. A good accent plant for the patio. Put indoors in winter.

Pentas, the Egyptian Star Flower, is new. Many fine varieties are sold; star-shaped flowers and dark green fuzzy leaves. Grows well with bright light, lots of water. Put two or three plants to a large white tub for a real display. Winter Pentas indoors.

Plumbago Capensis survives almost any situation. With small leaves and lovely blue flowers, it is almost ever blooming. Give it heavy watering, feeding. Hardy to 35 degrees.

Clerodendron Thompsoniae grows to about five feet. It has large ornamental dark green leaves, lovely white and red flowers. Wants a semi-shady spot. Good patio decoration. Grow indoors in winter.

Nerium Oleander is a graceful shrub to eight feet, at home on the patio. It has dark green leaves, many flowers. Single and double flowered forms in shades of white to pink to red to yellow. The plant takes buckets of water. Hardy to 20 degrees.

Tibouchinia semidecandra brings purple flowers to the patio. Fuzzy gray-green leaves. Needs some shade, heavy water.

Punica granatum nana, the dwarf pomegranate, is bushy and compact. Small green leaves, tiny orange fruits, not edible. Hardy to 25 degrees. Unusual, good.

SETTING A SHRUB OR TREE IN A TUB

It is wise to buy shrubs and trees from a nursery; they come either balled in burlap or in cans. If in cans, have the nurseyman cut each side. Water the plant thoroughly a day before planting it; if the root ball is dry the earth will break away from it when the can is pried loose. Set the slit can on its side and slide the root ball from it. Do not lift the plant by the trunk, rather cradle it in your arms and set it into the prepared container. If the plant is too low in the box, add more drainage materials and a layer of soil. If too high, tease away soil from the bottom of the roots. Fill in and around the root ball and sides of the tub with soil. Water thoroughly.

Before planting a balled burlap tree or shrub, soak it in water for a few hours. Then lower it into the tub on a bed of prepared soil and pack the soil in the void between the root ball and the sides of the tub to about ½ full. Soak it with water and then fill in with more soil. Before covering over the base of the shrub, cut the string around the burlap. In time the material will decompose in the soil.

There are many fine varieties of Ixora hybrids.   Pentas offer vivid color, red, orange, or pink.

Citrus tree growing in oil can at florist. Have nurserymen cut the can's sides.

Use a soil mix that meets the requirements of the plant being potted. Most trees grow well in a basic greenhouse soil. Some shrubs require additional acidity. (This information with plant descriptions). In wooden containers the soil stays cool and does not dry out as rapidly as plants in clay pots.

Some shrubs like Hibiscus and Clerodendron do fine with copious watering, others need a somewhat dry soil. When watering be sure the plant is thoroughly wet. Excess water should drain out the bottom holes. Weather and the position of the container—in shade or direct sun—dictate the watering schedule.

FOLIAGE PLANTS

Lush green leaves, attractive textures, pleasing patterns, are foliage plants. The philodendron, although definitely having its place on the patio or terrace, has finally been challenged by plants like diffenbachia, dracaena and caladium with different tones of leaf color. Texture too and leaf form vary greatly. Some have a sculptured look while others are massive and still others, delicate and airy.

There are many new foliage plants for the gardener. Make selection carefully so

In potting an azalea standard, oil can container is cut down both sides and removed. Prepare new container, insert plant, water well.

Kumquat in a planting box on a pebble terrace, top left. Bamboo plants in soy tubs, above. An elephant ear plant, left, complements tall units.

Trees in nursery are planted in burlap-wrapped balls. Photo below shows root ball in wrapping.

Two small ground trees and borders of ivy make this brick terrace a very handsome looking patio area.

that the plants you choose complement your outdoor setting. Specimen plants are available from many sources. One company lists 30 different kinds of philodendrons, a dozen aglaonemas; another nursery specializes in aralias. Many new exotic plants have finally made their debut.

FOLIAGE PLANTS FOR THE PATIO

Aralia (*fatsia japonica*) is a lush foliage plant with fan-shaped deeply lobed leaves. Grow it in partial shade; keep on the dry side. Hardy to 15 degrees.

Bamboo (*Phyllostachys Aurea*) is Golden Bamboo and grows 8 to 10 feet; a splendid vertical accent. Hedge bamboo (*Bambusa Multiplex*) also does well in containers. Grow both bamboos with plenty of water

and some sunlight. Hardy to 20 degrees.

Caladiums, striking large leaved plants are known for their magnificent colored leaves. Most of the plants sold are hybrids of *C. bicolor*. These are low growing plants and three or four to a white container, round or square, are handsome. Grow *caladiums* warm, minimum 68 degrees; they do equally well in sun or shade. In fall, the plants rest and when growth has stopped, remove the tubers from the pot and store in a shady cool place for a few months. They can be potted again in early spring.

Crotons (*Codiaeum variegatum*) are inexpensive and colorful. Grown to specimen size they have flashy red foliage in sunlight. Give them redwood tubs for a colorful display. Grows well with copious watering and then a drying out of the soil. Move indoors in winter.

Dracaena Marginata has long graceful branches topped with clusters of spear-shaped leaves, edged red. With sculptural effect, this dracaena is truly a dazzling sight. Keep the plant somewhat dry all year, spray the foliage and don t disturb the roots; top-dress rather than repot. A large Italian pot without a rim is an ideal container for this one. *D fragrans massangeana* is excellent too. It is a flowing cascade of yellow and green striped leaves. Handsome in a round soy tub or keg. Prune this dracaena occasionally and in a few years you will have a small tree. *D. phrynioid s* with long tapered dark green glossy leav s on arching stems is delicate, beautiful. It is well suited for that porcelain jardiniere. Move dracaenas indoors in winter unless you are in year-round temperate climate.

Ficus pandurata, the fiddle leaf fig from China, is a dramatic showpiece for a room

Citrus trees below. Many varieties are available.

Loquat tree in nursery, an amenable patio plant.

Dieffenbachia is a lush tropical American plant.

One of many Philodendrons;
make excellent patio plants.

One of popular Camellias,
left; make good tub plants.

Penthouse terrace has carefully balanced plantings.

Molly Adams

Fuchsias, camellias and other select shrubs surround this intimate patio in a natural, casual fashion.

Pittisporum makes an excellent corner subject.   Acer palmatum, Japanese maple; favorite subject.

Large plants, fountain, vines, fencing combine to turn city back yard into a quietly peaceful place.

or an outdoor area. The large dark green spoonshaped leaves grow quickly up a central stalk. Grow this plant in an acid soil and keep the foliage washed. This is a real show-off so use a plain round tub for it. Minimum night temperature: 60 degrees.

New Zealand Flax (*Phormium Tenax*), with sword-like leaves in fan pattern is one of the finest sculptural plants. There are many varieties sold. Some with bronze foliage, others dark green. Excellent for patio. Hardy to 20 degrees.

Philodendron pertusum, the "Swiss Cheese" plant, has mammoth scalloped leaves; popular for indoor and outdoor decoration. Repot it every year if you want lush growth. *P. radiatum*—is a smaller plant with dark green arrow-shaped leaves; handsome, easier to grow than most philodendrons. These are a few of the many in this family for patio growing. Minimum night temperature: 56 degrees.

Pittisporum tobira is a fine low bushy plant for long planters; three or four make a lush display. With glossy green leaves in clusters, it likes to be reasonably wet at all times. You might also want to try a single pot at floor level; in that case, use standard clay pots. Winter indoors.

Podocarpus nagi and *P. macrophylla* in wooden tubs, preferably hexagonal are five vertical accent decoration. Both are delicate and airy in appearance and need warmth and humidity. Minimum night temperature: 60 degrees. •

Best of the Flowering Plants

Flowering plants supply the melody in orchestrating your patio theme.

FOLIAGE plants are lovely but flowering plants are better. The colorful blossoms are bright and cheery; happy things to have outdoors. Where years ago, only a handful were available now there are hundreds to choose from.

ORCHIDS

Topping the list is orchids. These splendid plants, unique in the flower kingdom have finally taken their rightful place as house plants and to some extent as garden subjects. For the patio there are many of them that are grown easier than most plants and give harvests of beautiful flowers. Certainly, they deserve a place on the patio.

Selection in this plant group is vital.

Patio room with orchid plants. Orchids are popular because they'll bloom in each of the four seasons.

Basically, orchids can be divided into two groups: cool growing, warm growing. The cool kinds, those that grow in forty degree temperatures are ideal for outdoor growing in suitable containers. Warm orchids are fine for protected atriums or solariums. Where once only the popular types like Cattleyas and Cymbidiums were offered, now many different species are listed in suppliers catalogues. The choice depends on your own individual conditions. If you have a sunny place with cool nights select orchids from the Miltonia, Odontoglossum and Coelogyne families. For warm locations there are the Vandas, Aerides, Oncidiums and others.

Because orchids are flowers of the four seasons—plants bloom in spring, summer, fall and winter—they are immensely desirable. In most parts of the country you can have the spring, summer and early fall blooming plants. Bear in mind you want orchids that will flower; only a few are decorative without bloom.

The majority of orchids are either terrestrial (earth growing) or epiphytic (air borne). The terrestrials grow in soil as most other plants do. The epiphytes which are in the majority cling to tree branches. Both types require a special flower pot that has slots on the sides to permit circulation of air around the roots. You will also need packages of osmunda or fir bark sold at garden centers. The bark can be used as it comes from the package. The osmunda needs overnight soaking in water so you can cut it into small chunks for pot-

ting. Use either material by itself for epiphytes. For the terrestrials, combine one-part leaf mold and one-part chopped osmunda with one part commercial humus.

Because water must not linger at roots, make sure drainage is perfect when potting orchids. Break up old flower pots to provide you with shards to spread over the base of the pot. Be sure all materials are clean. Fill each pot to one-third full with shards. Then set the orchid plant in place and fill in and around with osmunda or bark or the mixture for the terrestrials. Press the material down with a short piece of blunt wood. Work from the sides to the center until you have firmly filled the pots to within half-an-inch of the rim. Leave this space to receive water.

When you place your orchid plants make arrangements for bottom ventilation. Orchids unlike other plants will not thrive set in saucers directly on the floor. Use florist wire stands (inexpensive at garden centers) or devise wood slat platforms for them. Or buy orchid hangers that clip onto pot rim and suspend plants from eyehooks in the ceiling. Hanging baskets of orchids really give a patio that glamorous look.

Some orchids need lots of sun, others do just fine in bright light and some want shady locations. In patio or terrace, creating humidity for the plants is done for you. The brick or concrete floor wet in the mornings creates humidity and many plants growing together will keep a safe amount of water in the air, about 50%.

Pendent flowering cool growing orchid, Coelogyne massangeana. It'll grow in shade, needs water all year.

Many orchids grow to great size. Do not be afraid to buy them. They will not perish over the winter; merely move them to an interior sunny spot. Or if your area has a roof they can be left outdoors where temperatures do not go below fifty degrees. Of all plants, orchids adjust to varying conditions and once accustomed to their new homes, make lavish displays. A Dendrobium orchid with 100 flowers is suitable decoration for the best patio.

If you are going to winter your plants indoors it is best to select species that normally are dormant in the dull season.

ORCHIDS FOR PATIOS

Orchids for growing from May to late

Laelia anceps with large ¾" rose-purple flowers.

September that I have tried and tested and are fool-proof:

Aerdies crispum, 2 to 5 feet tall has dark green leaves with delightfully scented 2-inch flowers. They are white flushed with rose, rose tipped, the lip rosy purple. A mature plant bears about thirty flowers in summer. Grow this orchid with copious moisture except in winter when bark should become dry between waterings. Needs sun, minimum night temperature: 56 degrees F.

Bifrenaria tyrianthina is about 24 inches tall with large flowers of reddish purple, the lip colored with deeper veins. Grow the plant on the cool side (54 to 58 F. at night) and with two to three hours of filtered sun rather than direct sunshine. Pot it in fir bark; will have to be grown at a sunny window during the winter, put outside for patio bloom in May. After it flowers allow it a dry rest for about a month. When new growth appears resume watering. Even without bloom this is a decorative small orchid for patio growing.

Coelogyne massangeana, is a handsome plant to about 30 inches; the leaves are broad, pale green, somewhat like the plantain lily. The flowers are produced on a pendent scape sometimes as many as thirty or forty to a stem. They are one inch across, snow white, with brown markings. Pot this orchid in large containers of fir bark; it needs water all year. Provide adequate humidity about 50 per cent. Will grow in filtered sun or in shade.

Dendrobium Dalhousieanum is one of the fine 'Dendrobes' sometimes called the nobile group. These plants require cool temperature (49 to 54 degrees, night), during the winter months. Give them as much sun as possible and keep the fir bark on the dry side. When warm weather starts they can be moved to the patio, watering resumed, for spring bloom. *D. Dalhousieanum* has tall canes with 5 inch tawny beige flowers marked with maroon. *D. Pierardi* has 2 inch blush pink flowers and *D. Superbum* bears large lilac flowers rhubarb scented on 5 to 6 foot canes.

Epidendrum o'brienianum has 1 inch flowers in summer clustered at the top of the growth. Many varieties are available and colors range from pink to lavendar to red. Needs sunlight and warmth, (minimum 62 degrees F. at night). Give it plenty of water; a good vertical plant for corner accent.

Laelia Anceps grows to about 30 inches

and bears 3 to 4 inch rose purple flowers. This splendid orchid needs cool nights (56 degrees F.). Grow the plant in fir bark kept moderately moist all year. Will want some sunshine.

Laelia Gouldiana, a somewhat smaller plant produces 2 inch dark rose flowers, many to a terminal raeceme. Grow it the same as L. Anceps.

Lycaste Aromatica with light green foliage has 1 inch brilliant yellow blooms. Needs bright light rather than sun and a decided rest (about a month) before and after flowering. Usually spring blooming.

Lycaste Deppi, a medium size plant has large flowers of pale green flushed with red, the lip pure white. Grow it in fir bark in a bright location.

Odontoglossum Grande is the popular tiger orchid with large, 5 to 7 inch yellow and brown flowers in autumn. A good one to grow that requires minimum care; bright light, moderate waterings, and large grade fir bark.

Odontoglossum Citrosmum wants cool nights (45 degrees F.). A medium size plant it has fragrant frilly white flowers with light pink or purple at the base of the lip. Good for window trays and shelves. Summer blooming.

Oncidium bictoniese, a fine plant that blooms from August to October grows about 40 inches tall. The 1 inch flowers are on branched erect scapes, pink and brown. Some sun, cool evenings.

Phaius grandifolius produces yellow and

Closeup view of tuberous begonia, among the most colorful and popular of the summer flowering plants.
Antonelli Bros.

ORCHID POTTING WITH FIR BARK

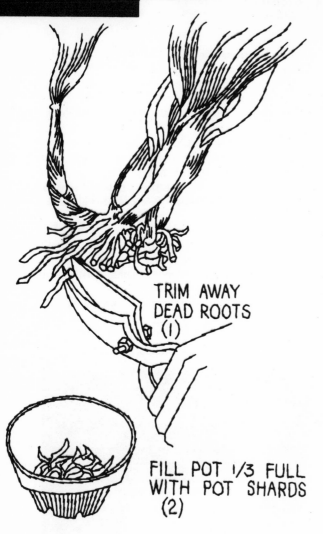

TRIM AWAY
DEAD ROOTS
(1)

FILL POT 1/3 FULL
WITH POT SHARDS
(2)

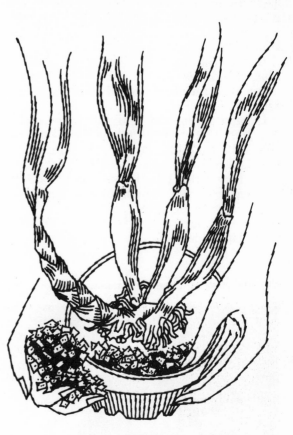

FILL AROUND ROOT
BALL WITH FIR BARK
(3)

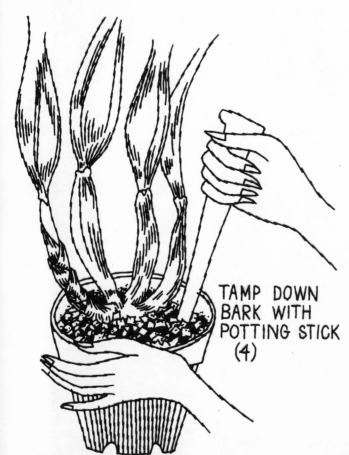

TAMP DOWN
BARK WITH
POTTING STICK
(4)

TIE AND STAKE
PLANT, LABEL
(5)

Cattleya species orchid
in bloom is dazzling.

Spring flowering pink
Dendrobium pierardii.

brown flowers in summer. The foliage is dark green and handsome. Wants some shade; grows well warm or cool.

Miltonia spectabilis is showy with large solitary flowers with creamy white sepals and petals and a broad rose-purple lip edged with pale rose. Grow it cool and shady. Usually summer blooming.

Sobralia macrantha, a handsome plant even out of bloom with light green ribbed leaves bears large crimson purple flowers. Needs sun and plenty of water. Pot in terrestrial mix. Not fussy about temperature.

Vanda coerulea produces pale blue flowers late fall. They are 4 inches across. Likes coolness and some bright light, heavy watering.

GINGER FAMILY

The genera ginger covers several groups of plants with foliage similar to the banana family. They are basically reed-like plants with blade shaped leaves and stout stalks. Some are short, others grow to fifteen feet. There is red ginger, shell ginger, spiral ginger, white ginger, torch ginger and many others. Some are listed in catalogues, others are still to come. The flowers are incredible; brightly colored bracts that seem lacquered, unreal they are so brilliant.

Most gingers need a rich loamy soil laced with bonemeal. Give them plenty of water and as much sunlight as possible. Unlike banana plants, ginger will tolerate cool evenings (45 degrees). If you are not in temperate year round climate, take gingers inside during the winter. Put them at a sunny window; during the dull season keep the soil just barely wet.

This group of plants has been completely overlooked by gardeners and certainly deserves more attention. They are no more difficult to grow than any other plant and to me, give much more of a reward. Spray

ORCHID POTTING WITH OSMUNDA

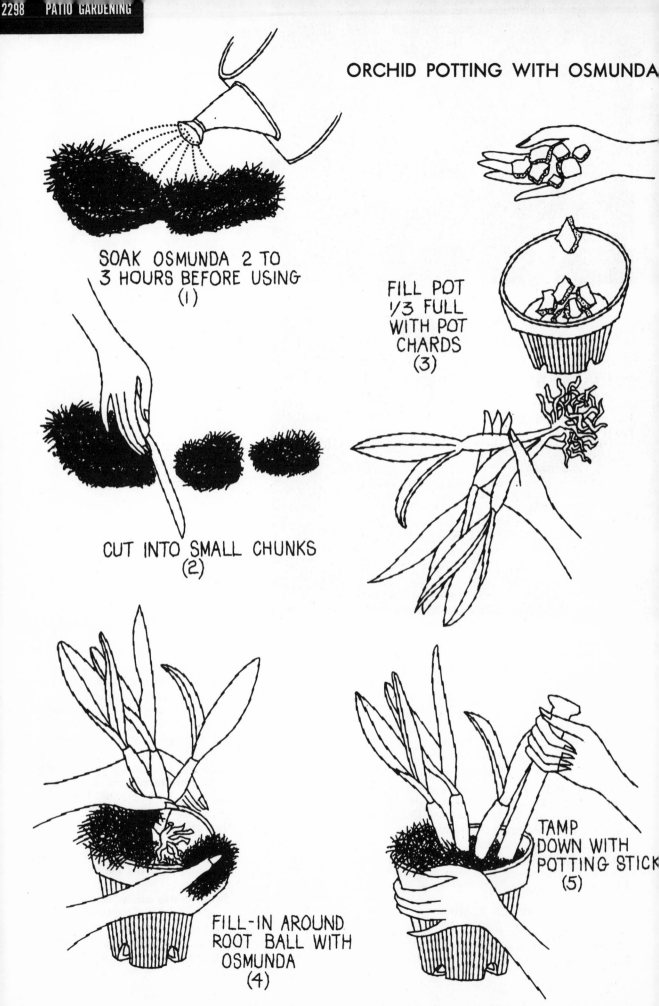

SOAK OSMUNDA 2 TO
3 HOURS BEFORE USING
(1)

CUT INTO SMALL CHUNKS
(2)

FILL POT
1/3 FULL
WITH POT
CHARDS
(3)

FILL-IN AROUND
ROOT BALL WITH
OSMUNDA
(4)

TAMP
DOWN WITH
POTTING STICK
(5)

Mrs. Carl Meyer

Camellia type tuberous begonia has large blooms in typical colors. Ruffled form is fluted at edges.

the plants daily to keep up humidity and keep a watchful eye for insects. If they do attack the plants, use a malathion insecticide.

SUMMER FLOWERING GINGERS

Some ginger plants for outdoor areas:

Hedychium coronarium, Butterfly Lily, has pure white flowers leafy canes to 6 feet long. Grow in large pots of rich soil with sunlight, heavy watering.

Alpinia purpurata with floral heads growing at the end of the leafstalk may be a foot or more long. It has large open vivid red bracts, the tiny white flowers hidden inside. A real show in bloom.

Alpinia nutans has pendant clusters of white flowers, marked yellow and red. This plant is big, to 10 feet with alternate leaf blades.

Phaemoria magnifica, Torch Ginger produces a spectacular flower. It is shaped like a torch, sometimes 8 inches across, brilliant red surrounded by scalelike formation. The bracts hide the true yellow flowers. Sun, warmth and heavy watering.

Hedychium gardnerianum produces green bracts and yellow flowers lined red. They are fragrant. Grows well cool.

Costus igneus, a small plant for shelf or tray bears ruffled fringed flowers. The leaves of the plant curve spurally and are not as long or as bladelike as other gingers. Needs shade, plenty of water and warmth.

THE BANANA FAMILY

Heliconias, striking plants with vivid colored inflorescence are relatives of the banana. Most are large with spoon shaped leaves but there are also some smaller types. The flower head resembles the bromeliad bloom; the bracts holding the true flowers. The plants have names like Lobster Claw, Parrot Plant and Bird of Paradise.

These plants need warmth, 60 degrees F. at night, and plenty of water during the growing season. Grow them in large pots with a rich soil kept almost constantly moist. Give them some sunlight and keep the foliage misted. A healthy plant sprouts seven or eight leaves in a season so be sure you have the space before selecting these splendid plants.

Because Heliconias naturally die down in winter they make ideal patio subjects. Simply store them without water during the dull season and then start them again in early spring. Usually my plants tell me when it's time to start watering them again. Small green shoots appear in early April.

The blossoms on the plant last about a week and you might want to cut some for a unique flower arrangement.

SUMMER BLOOMING HELICONIAS

Heliconia angustifolia, with stalks about 3 feet high and leathery leaves bears orange-red bracts with creamy white flowers.

Heliconia humilis, the Lobster Claw derives the name from a series of bracts, the color of a boiled lobster. Each claw may be 5 inches long. Another large plant.

Heliconia aurantiaca, about 3 feet high bearing smooth leathery leaves with erect

Yellow Stanhopea orchid for late summer color.

Lycaste orchid grows easily, needs bright light.

orange bracts tipped green. A startling plant in bloom.

Strelitzia reginae, the popular Bird of Paradise with orange and blue bracts on tall erect stems. Spoon shaped dark green leaves. Only plants with seven or more leaves bloom.

Heliconia psittacorum, smaller, is often called the Parrot flower and resembles the Bird of Paradise. It has leathery rich green leaves and shining orange inflorescence.

Heliconia latispatha has boat shaped orange yellow bracts well above the dark green foliage.

Heliconia elongata bears green, yellow and pink bracts; similar to Lobster Claw Plant. One of the earliest flowering of this group.

TUBEROUS BEGONIAS

Begonias with tuberous roots have gained world-wide recognition and rightly so. They are superalative flowering plants. In full bloom they are a sight to behold, a veritable sea of color. It is hard to find a summer flower for patio and terrace better than tuberous begonias.

Today's tuberous begonias properly called tuber hybrida are intercrossed hybrids bred to near perfection in flower form, size and color. They bloom profusely in all colors except blue. Whether in single pots or grouped together in planters they add the magic note to an outdoor area.

In March, select large or middle size tubers—those an inch or more in diameter —from reputable dealers. Put a 2 inch layer of peat moss and sand (1 to 2 ratio) in a wooden flat or other suitable box. Set the tubers 2 inches apart and about ½ inch deep with the dented side up, in the medium. Cover them with about ¼ inch of the mix. Roots develop from bottom, sides and top so be sure the tuber is covered. Place the flat in good light in 60 to 70 degree F. and keep the rooting medium barely wet. Too much water causes the tubers to rot. When the sprouts are about 2 inches tall (about two weeks) shift them to shallow pots. I use a 4 inch azalea pot with a layer of stone and loose soil. (2 parts loam to 1 part leaf mold.) Move the potted begonias to a cooler place. Water them sparingly and watch for mildew or mealy bugs.

In a few weeks, around the middle of May, begonias will be larger but still in shallow pots. Put them on the patio for summer bloom. If plants develop too fast and become too large before danger of frost is past, they can be held back by cool temperatures. Or if they are not growing fast enough, warmth will accelerate growth.

Tuberous begonias do best in pots placed on patio floor or in hanging containers where air circulates around the basket. Like the orchids from countries of high altitude, tuberous begonias need good air circulation. There is a standard metal pot clip (available at nurseries) that attaches to brick or wood walls. It has a metal grasping devise that holds the rim of the pot. These are unique hangers, neat and simple and take only a few minutes to install. Bracket and pot units are good too. The bracket attaches to the wall and the arm or pot holder swivels so a plant can be placed at any desired angle. Baskets suspended from porch rafters or lattice work are excellent. These wire baskets have open spaces and air circulates freely through the growing medium. Line the baskets with sheet moss. Wooden tubs and boxes are other suitable containers. They hold moisture, look good and last a lifetime.

Place your plants where there is some scattered sunshine. Tuberous begonias survive heat during the day but must have cool nights, 55 to 60 F. If summer days are very hot, mist the area around the plants (not the leaves). Water begonias heavily on bright days, not so much in cloudy weather. When they are growing well, start using a fertilizer mixed half-strength every second week.

After flowering, when leaves turn dry and yellow, water sparingly but let growth continue for as long as possible. Then take the pots inside. Lift the tubers and wash and dry them thoroughly. Store them in shallow boxes—I put them in metal baking dishes—at 45 to 50 F. Give them good air circulation but no light. Keep them dry until next spring.

FLOWER FORM BEGONIAS

Camelliaeflora, most often seen, has a flat flower with incredibly large blooms in all typical colors. The ruffled form is fluted and frilled at the edges. There are endless varieties.

Fimbriata has frayed petals resembling carnations. These are robust bloomers with large leaves and erect flowers.

Cristata flowers are big, single with a

Calif. Redwood Assoc.
Strelizia reginae, known as Bird of Paradise.

tufted crest on each petal, often a different color than the petal itself.

Marginata flowers have two forms: *Crispa marginata,* frilled singles with the same color edges and *Double marginata* with petals lined and edged with bands of contrasting colors.

Picotee has petals lined with another color bleeding into the dominant flower color. There are picotees in camellia and rose form too.

Rose form has a high center of petals inside, and outer petals flared back like a rose.

Narcissiflora has the center of the flower shaped like a trumpet.

Named varieties include:

'Ballerina'—a beautiful double ruffled form.

'Black Knight'—spectacular deep crimson flowers.

'Bonanza'—ruffled golden apricot, blooms 7 to 9 inches across. From Vetterle and Reinelt, Capitola, California.

'Chinook'—rose form with flowers 6 to 8 inches across, pure salmon color. From Vetterle and Reinelt, Capitola, California.

Clay pots keep begonias cooler and healthier.   Summer white, yellow Dendrobium thyrsiflorum.

Tuberous begonias for outdoor summer color. Plants comes in all shades of pink, red and yellow.

Mrs. Carl Meyer

Mature specimen tuberous begonia. Always put them in patio area with maximum air circulation.

'Flambeau'—lovely double orange flowers.

'Frances Powell'—a nice double pink flowers.

'Gaucho'—mammoth ruffled flowers of a deep orange. From Vetterle and Reinelt, Capitola, California.

'Mandarin'—double salmon orange blooms.

'Rosado'—deeply frilled and ruffled pink blooms. From Vetterle and Reinelt, Capitola, California.

'Royal Flush'—a brilliant scarlet form of exceptional beauty. Vetterle and Reinelt, Capitola, California.

FUCHSIAS

Close behind tuberous begonias for a grand display of color are fuchsias. In full bloom in August and September they are tough plants to beat. And once the cuttings are started or young plants bought at nurseries they are easy to handle. You can grow them indoors to get them started or if you are in favored climate put them on the patio immediately. Give them a good soil with plenty of leaf mold, keep them well watered and in a bright place. I cannot stress too strongly the need of heavy watering for fuchsias. Also important is light; fuchsias will not bloom in complete shade.

For the most part, fuchsias are hanging basket plants; a well grown specimen will be so covered with bloom it is hard to see the container. If you do not have appropriate places for hanging baskets on the patio—posts, brackets, ceilings—put them on shelves or simply against the house wall. Some wooden containers have one flat side for this type of hanging.

FOR BASKET-GROWING TRY:

'Cascade'—carmine and white.
'Cavalier'—pink and purple.
'Creole'—crimson and maroon.
'Golden Marinka'—red.
'Pebble Beach'—white, rose, purple.
'Tiffany'—snow white.

Although fuchsias perhaps look best as basket plants they can also be used as hedges or for summer bedding. Or they can be grown in espalier form or for pyramid tub growing. This is a versatile family, so choose the variety for the kind of growing you have in mind.

FOR HEDGES

'Corallina'—scarlet and purple.
'Heritage'—scarlet and purple.
'Prodigy'—cerise and royal purple.
'Tresco'—red and purple.

FOR SUMMER BEDDING

'Brilliant'—scarlet and violet magenta.
'Charming'—carmine and reddish-purple.
'Elsa'—ivory pink and rose purple.
'Grenadier'—scarlet and purple.

Odontoglossum grande has yellow, brown flowers.

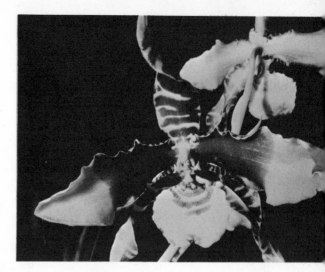

Antonelli Bros.

Epidendrum species spray-type orchid needs sun.

Sobralia orchid bears large rose-purple flowers.

PYRAMID TUB GROWING

'Coquette'—white, red and purple.
'Morning Mist'—orange-rose and purple.
'San Francisco'—carmine.
'Swingtime'—red and white.

MULTIFLORAS

The Multifloras are a smaller group of summer flowering tuberous begonias, compact in growth with many flowers, either single or semidouble. They are good as garden borders or as window sill plants. Easier to grow than other tuberous kinds, the multifloras tolerate more sun and less humidity.

Some named varieties you might want to try:

'Copper Gold'—double gold.
'Flamboy ante'—single scarlet.
'Helen Harms'—double yellow.
'Rambouillet'—semidouble red.
'Sweet Home'—double red.
'Tasso'—semidouble pink.
'William Eysser'—semidouble deep salmon.

PENDULAS

Pendulas are trailing tuberous begonias listed in catalogues as hanging basket or Lloydi types. They are stunning decoration with cascades of colorful flowers. . . . They bloom a long time, into fall and need warmth and humidity and protection from the wind and sun.

Pinch out young shoots early in the season to promote pendent growth.

Here are some varieties to try:

'Cherie'—Rose form, salmon rose color.
'Illumination'—Rose form, double.
'Pink Shower'—Lovely clear pink flowers.
'Wild Rose'—Deep pink, 4 to 5-inches across. •

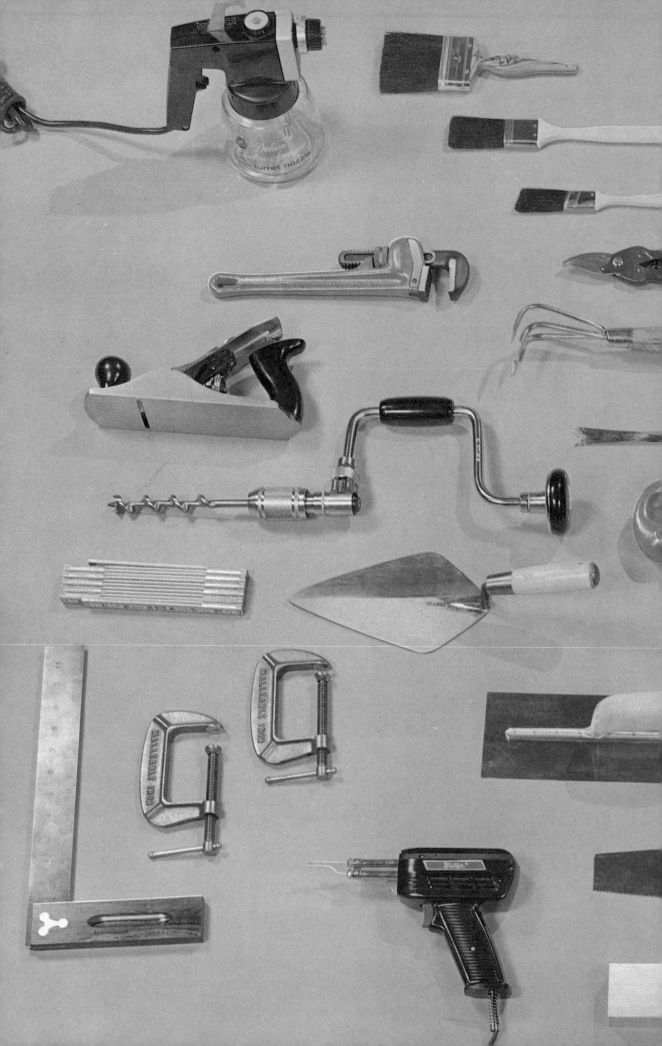